T0114833

THE POWER
OF TEAM
LEADERSHIP

BARNA REPORTS *for* HIGHLY EFFECTIVE CHURCHES

THE POWER OF TEAM LEADERSHIP

Achieving Success Through

Shared Responsibility

Previously released as *Building Effective Lay Leadership Teams*

GEORGE BARNA

President, Barna Research Group, Ltd.

WATERBROOK
PRESS

THE POWER OF TEAM LEADERSHIP
PUBLISHED BY WATERBROOK PRESS
12265 Oracle Boulevard, Suite 200
Colorado Springs, Colorado 80921

All Scripture quotations, unless otherwise indicated, are taken from the *Holy Bible, New International Version®*. NIV®. Copyright © 1973, 1978, 1984 by International Bible Society. Used by permission of Zondervan Publishing House. All rights reserved. Scripture quotations marked (KJV) are taken from the *King James Version.* Scripture quotations marked (TLB) are taken from *The Living Bible* copyright © 1971. Used by permission of Tyndale House Publishers, Inc., Wheaton, Illinois 60189. All rights reserved.

Trade Paperback ISBN 978-0-7352-8973-4
Hardcover ISBN 978-1-57856-424-8
eBook ISBN 978-0-307-83123-1

Published in association with Sealy M. Yates, Literary Agent, Orange, California.

Published in the United States by WaterBrook Multnomah, an imprint of the Crown Publishing Group, a division of Penguin Random House LLC, New York.

WATERBROOK and its deer colophon are registered trademarks of Penguin Random House LLC.

Library of Congress Cataloging-in-Publication Data

Barna, George.
  The power of team leadership : achieving success through shared responsibility / by George Barna.
      p. cm. — (Barna reports for highly effective churches series)
  Includes bibliographical references.
  ISBN 1-57856-424-7
      1. Group ministry. I. Title.

BV675 .B37 2001
253—dc21   2001039002

Previously released in a slightly different version by Issachar Resources under the title *Building Effective Lay Leadership Teams.*

CONTENTS

———◆◆◆———

CHAPTER ONE

ARE WE SETTING UP PASTORS —AND CHURCHES—FOR FAILURE?

The problem is not our leaders but the unhealthy expectations we have of them.

Most of us have bought into an unhealthy understanding of leadership.

We have been taught that leadership is about one individual's performing all of an organization's critical tasks—motivating, mobilizing, directing, and resourcing people to fulfill a vision—at a level of excellence and influence that separates him or her from the bulk of humanity. The combination of skills and abilities required to be a great leader has caused many people to lament the absence of leaders in our society.

Let me share why I believe we have unrealistic expectations for our leaders. In a nationwide survey we conducted among 1,005 adults, people identified those things they feel are "very important" for a leader to do. Here is the profile:

- 87 percent expect leaders to motivate people to get involved in meaningful causes and activity

- 78 percent believe leaders should negotiate compromises and resolve conflicts when they arise

- 77 percent look to leaders to determine and convey the course of action that people should take in order to produce desirable conditions and outcomes

- 76 percent rely on leaders to identify and implement courses of action that are in the best interests of society, even if some of those choices are unpopular

- 75 percent expect leaders to invest their time and energy in training more leaders who will help bring the vision to reality

- 63 percent want leaders to communicate vision so that they know where things are headed and what it will take to get there

- 61 percent say leaders are responsible for the direction and production of employees associated with the leader's organization or cause

- 61 percent think leaders should analyze situations and create the strategies and plans that direct the resources of those who follow them

- 56 percent hold leaders responsible for managing the day-to-day details of the operation.[1]

The list goes on, but it clearly shows that we have developed an unreasonable notion of what a leader should do. Look at the breadth of tasks and abilities demanded by the expectations reflected in that survey—and realize, of course, that most people hold additional expectations beyond those listed. We expect the central leader not only to provide the corporate vision, but also to:

- direct activity

- encourage participants

- supply resources

- evaluate plans and progress

- motivate participants

- negotiate agreements

- strategize

- manage people

- reinforce commitments

- recruit necessary colleagues

- communicate conditions, plans, and assignments

- train new leaders

- resolve conflicts

- and so on

Who could possibly meet such a wide range of disparate expectations?

SET UP FOR FAILURE

Would you agree that a person would have to be superhuman to accomplish all of these tasks? Yet that's what we expect a leader to do. No wonder we are consistently disappointed by leaders who seemed to hold such promise before they assumed positions of significant authority and responsibility. Our surveys have shown that during the past two decades there has been a continual decline in satisfaction with leadership in churches, government, nonprofit organizations, schools, businesses, and families.

When you reach a point of frustration or incapacity, one useful strategy is to go back and question your assumptions to determine if they were errant and therefore contributed to the blockage. If we take that approach to our consternation regarding leadership, we will most likely conclude that the real problem is not our leaders but the unhealthy expectations we have of them. Few men or women have the individual capacity to deliver all that we have come to expect of those in positions of authority. We set leaders up for failure by holding them to absurd performance standards. We set organizations up for failure by intimately tying the success and well-being of the institution to the quality of leadership it receives. We set people up for frustration, disappointment, and failure by basing their present and future well-being upon the capacity of the individual leader whom they most closely follow in any given dimension of their lives.

OPTIONS FOR IMPROVEMENT

Once we understand the problem, there are several options we might consider for improving the situation—some good, some not so good.

First, we could accept the situation as a reality that is certainly imperfect but cannot and will not change. From that perspective, our responsibility is simply to make the best of it. No matter how many superior scenarios we dream up, we might assume that they are not likely to become reality, so we feel we might as well not tantalize ourselves with unrealistic potentials. While such an analysis may have some appeal, it is undoubtedly a defeatist, lazy-minded perspective. It is hard to imagine any scenario in life in which improvements are impossible.

Second, we could argue that the real problem is our failure to identify the most qualified leaders. If we could get those people in place, things would improve. This is a common complaint heard within the political arena: The system and the election process scare away the most capable and qualified candidates, leaving only those so desperate for the job that they will do whatever it takes to win elected office. Once again, this view is not very realistic. True leaders rarely shrink from a reasonable challenge, especially if one of their potential accomplishments is changing the system to facilitate better outcomes and to make the task more attractive to other leaders.

Third, we might posit that past and present leaders have failed to meet our expectations because they have not been adequately trained. This notion is undermined by ample evidence that suggests our leaders often receive the best training available, whether in school, in the field, or through mentoring. Effective leaders have many traits—among them a strong desire to succeed—that often drive them to gain the training, information, experience, and skills needed to accomplish their goals. While there are many examples we could cite of leaders not having enough training, this explanation appears insufficient to describe the existing dearth of effective leaders, especially in our churches.

Finally, a wiser alternative, in my view, would be to accept the fact that the current system does not work because it has an inherent flaw in its foundation that must be addressed. Such broad thinking opens up a world of possibilities and conjecture. What hypotheses are worth testing? If we were to build the "ideal model" of leadership, regardless of what models now prevail, what would that model look like? Working backward from a clear-cut notion of "effective leadership," what would we strive to facilitate? In other words, rather than try to enable existing leaders to live up to the extremely high levels of performance we demand of them, how could we reconceptualize and innovatively redefine the leadership process?

TEAMS TO THE RESCUE

Let me confess that it took me a long time to realize that the first three options described above—that is, accepting things as they are, recruiting better-quality leaders, and providing leaders with better training—will not necessarily produce the results we are seeking. As a product of the institutions and methods that produced the problem in the first place, I had been completely blinded to alternatives to the leader-as-superstar approach.

Over the past two years I have had the privilege of discovering what many other people already knew and practiced: Leadership works best when it is provided by teams of gifted leaders serving together in pursuit of a clear and compelling vision.

In the past decade, more than four thousand new books on leadership have been published. Most discuss the indispensable skills needed to become king of the hill; few downplay personal superiority or emphasize serving within a team context. Almost every leadership book or training course discusses what the central leader can do to satisfy people's demands and outperform everyone else; rarely do leadership books or courses dare to suggest that leadership is best accomplished without a high-profile, multitalented, popular icon in the center-stage spotlight. But we have found that the "superstar" model of leadership, while appealing and not without some experiential validity, can do more to decimate the health of an organization than to facilitate its well-being.

Leadership works best when it is provided by teams of gifted leaders serving together in pursuit of a clear and compelling vision.

After years of conducting research and analysis for government agencies, political leaders, Fortune 500 corporations, nonprofit organizations, and churches, I am convinced that the greatest challenges in our society stem from the absence of quality leadership. We live in an increasingly complex and sophisticated society. People are constantly bombarded by opportunities, challenges, and choices. No one can deny that we do, indeed, live in the land and age of opportunity.

But as human beings we are prone to chase outcomes that may not be realistic or even in our own best interests. Often we ignore the common good for the personal good. As often as not we make choices that we later regret or that reflect poor judgment. Making good choices, discerning appropriate priorities, and staying focused and on track is exceedingly difficult. What will enable us to make progress toward outcomes that honor God, improve people's quality of life, and facilitate joy and meaning?

Quality leadership.

But the answer does not lie in unearthing more superhero leaders who satisfy the grandiose, ever-expanding demands of the people. The answer lies in combining the talents of gifted leaders to create synergistic outcomes. Team leadership is the only approach that carries the promise of satisfying the needs of our society. Solo leaders will always have an important place in our present and future reality, but I believe that teams hold the key to the future.

THE IMPACT OF TEAM LEADERSHIP

In conversations with people, I have come to realize that we are not aware of just how much our lives have been impacted by leadership teams. Consider just a few examples that you may have overlooked.

- Major political decisions are made at both the federal and state levels by executives whom we have elected—specifically, by the president of the United States and by the governor of your state. But do you realize that those two individuals, while elected to lead, each rely heavily upon a cabinet—a small group of advisors who are leaders in their own right and who provide substantial input into the key strategic decisions made by the chief executive? It is the rare—and usually unsuccessful—government leader who makes important, life-impacting decisions without careful study and discussion among a handful of selected counselors whose experience, skills, and abilities complement those of the chief executive.

- Your physical safety has been sustained by the military. You may be aware that key military decisions are rarely the choice of one individual, such as a general, but they are the outcome of a small group of experienced, trained professionals who work together to make important decisions. At the policy-making level, we might identify the Joint Chiefs of Staff as such a leadership team. Within a given branch of the military there are other teams at work, enabling the chief leader of the branch to make significant decisions.

- Sports teams use multiple leaders to devise effective strategy, representing a team behind the scenes as well as the team that you enjoy watching on the field. In football, the head coach works with a team of assistant coaches including a defensive coach, an offensive coach, a special teams' coach, and a tactician who has studied the opponents to understand their strengths and weaknesses. In basketball you may have the head coach working in tandem with a coach of the guards, one who focuses on the forwards and centers, and another who tracks what the opponents have been doing. Baseball teams have coaches who help the manager by focusing on various functions such as hitting, pitching, scouting, and conditioning.

- The board of directors of many large corporations uses an "executive committee" that shapes policy and other core decisions for the corporation. That committee is usually a handful of people—from three to seven individuals—who assist the board chairperson in developing key outcomes. The team often includes individuals of divergent, complementary backgrounds covering areas such as finance, human resources, management, marketing, and technology.

A major advantage of being led by a team is that the results almost always transcend what any individual from that team could have produced alone.

Clearly, teams of leaders affect our lives every day. In many cases we may not realize the depth and range of leadership competence provided simply because a team works so smoothly—almost as if it were one indivisible entity rather than a collection of individuals. In these situations the team embraces one unified position, speaks with one voice, gains a single image in the public eye, and operates with such unity that we remain unaware of the multiple parts that work cooperatively behind the scenes. When those parts are working in lockstep, all we see—or care about—are the results. A major advantage of being led by a team is that the results almost always transcend what any individual from that team could have produced without the assistance of the other leaders involved in that team.

CHALLENGES FACING TODAY'S LEADERS

To sense the full impact of the importance of shifting from solo leadership to team leadership, take a moment to consider some of the challenges that face our culture today.

- *Population growth.* Already the third most-populated nation in the world, the United States will add another thirty million people to its population this decade. That growth will result in a wide variety of new pressures, needs, and expectations.

- *Morality.* One of the growing concerns of Americans is the moral and ethical decline of our nation. In a previous book I predicted that this would be the decade in which America would be overtaken by moral anarchy—an environment in which people do whatever they feel is in their personal interests regardless of the law, the common good, or the needs of the groups with which they are associated. While a remnant is deeply concerned about moral decay, most people have come to accept it and strive to cope with it—primarily by honing and excusing their own decadent practices.

- *Expectations.* People expect to have the best of everything at a low cost and delivered immediately. Having abandoned God as the center of our lives, we seek fulfillment from other sources, especially our material possessions and entertainment experiences. We resent anything that gets in the way of our being able to achieve maximum pleasure.

- *Families.* Soaring levels of divorce, "gay marriages," legal abortions, latchkey children, family poverty, in-home violence, and out-of-wedlock births among both adults and teenagers, combined with fewer mothers staying home to nurture young children and the declining quality of communication within families have made a pipe dream of the notion that the family is the primary delivery agent of appropriate values and behavior. Families themselves no longer turn inward for the direction and resources they need for maturation and quality of life; instead, they turn outward to get what they need, which leads to further weakening and disintegration of the family unit.

- *Values.* Traditional values such as absolute moral truth, personal integrity, and respect for authority have been twisted beyond recognition. The new values in place have reshaped our relationships with people and institutions.

The list of challenges facing leaders could go on for pages. (In my recent book, *Boiling Point,* I spend three hundred–plus pages detailing the changing nature of our society and its implications for leaders and churches.[2]) The severity of the cultural shifts we have witnessed in recent years emphasizes that one person is not likely to provide the breadth and acuity of leadership demanded by such an environment. Expecting any one individual to meet such extraordinary demands is not only naive, but borders on being cruel to the leader and unjust to the enterprise he or she leads.

SIX NEW LEADERSHIP TRENDS IN THE CHURCH

We continue examining the context in which leadership occurs by studying some of the shifts happening in churches. Consider the following six trends that are reshaping leadership in ministry:

1. *Increasing numbers of senior pastors are shifting from the role of preacher-counselor to that of leader-trainer.* Without diminishing the importance of preaching and counseling, there is a heightened realization that the congregation relies upon the senior pastor for vision, motivation, and mobilization. The result is a redefining of how pastors use their resources to have impact.

2. *Four forces are converging to change the role of the laity in leadership.* First, people are demanding participation in the development of their current experience and future

conditions. Second, Christians are becoming more aware of their spiritual gifts—and more eager to use those gifts in personal ministry and for the benefit of their church. Third, most of our seminaries are still oriented more toward producing preacher-counselors than toward training effective leader-trainers. As a result, many churches must look elsewhere for individuals who have been called by God to lead, have been trained to do so, and have solid leadership experience. Fourth, pastors are increasingly open to sharing the leadership of the church's ministry with competent and committed laity. The outgrowth of these new realities is that churches are identifying, training, and deploying congregants as key leaders within the ministry. Ministry leaders are increasingly being raised up from within the congregation instead of being chosen from résumés presented by outsiders.

3. *More churches are striving to accurately determine the health of their ministry.* To facilitate that transition, attention is being shifted from church growth—primarily qualitative in nature—to church health, which addresses ministry quality. This change in emphasis will necessarily demand a different leadership focus and new skills.

4. *In the past decade, the Holy Spirit has received greater attention and devotion than at any time in the past half-century.* One implication of this "comeback"

by the third Person of the Trinity is that church leaders must now consider the appropriate blending of business-oriented skills with sensitivity to the prompting of the Holy Spirit. This produces a better balance of head and heart in leading the ministry.

5. *Extensive research over more than three decades has confirmed the view that although leadership skills can be taught, leadership will always be an art, not a definable science.* As such, while methodology is important and techniques can be taught to bring about superior outcomes, the acceptance of leadership as a "soft science" frees churches to concentrate on leadership as a ministry rather than as a discipline that facilitates ministry. The bottom line is that leaders minister by serving others.

6. *Congregants demand excellence and relevance from their church.* This perspective has changed the way in which people want to be treated when they invest themselves in ministry. Rather than being described as volunteers, unpaid laypeople want to be regarded as "ministry professionals." Churches are changing the terms they use to describe volunteers and the quantity of resources made available to them, and they are providing different forms of supervision to these ministry partners. This alters how full-time church leaders perceive and carry out their work within the congregational context.

Each of these trends points to a meaningful shift in how people think, interact, work, and perceive ministry. When the context changes, leadership must adapt. The changes described above demand that leaders perform the same fundamental functions—giving people a sense of where to go and how to get there—but deliver the related resources in ways that fit the new cultural context.

PASTORS' SELF-PERCEPTIONS

Another key insight from our research is that most pastors neither see themselves as leaders nor aspire to be leaders. In a recent national survey of Protestant senior pastors, we asked them to identify their spiritual gifts. Only 12 percent said they have the gift of leadership. In contrast, two-thirds of pastors surveyed said they have the gift of teaching or preaching. They have accurately recognized that teaching and leading are two very distinct responsibilities and activities that require different skills that produce differing results.

> *Leadership will always be an art,
> not a definable science.*

Despite the trends highlighted above, the continuing, prevailing mind-set among pastors is that their primary job is to preach from the Bible and to take advantage of other opportunities to teach. Our studies have shown that there is a very high level of frustration among pastors: They went to seminary to learn how to preach and pastor, not how to lead—yet their people expect strong, visionary leadership in addition to practical, challenging, and life-changing teaching.

> *Less than one out of every ten senior pastors can articulate the vision for the ministry he or she leads.*

Another relevant finding from research we conducted several years ago is that less than one out of every ten senior pastors can articulate the vision for the ministry he or she is trying to lead. Combine pastors' personal convictions that they have not been called to lead with their inability to articulate God's vision for their ministry, and you can clearly see that we will be in trouble if we rely upon senior pastors to provide all or most of the leadership in our churches. A church can compensate for the absence of many skills and resources, but it cannot overcome the absence of effective leadership. If that leadership is not going to come from pastors, then it must come from somewhere else.

And that is where team leadership enters the picture.

CHAPTER TWO

WHY TEAM
LEADERSHIP?

*Are your church members
merely consuming ministry,
or are they doing ministry?*

Even though leadership plays such an integral role in every person's life, we throw the words "leader" and "leadership" around quite carelessly. Often you hear someone referred to as "a leader in her field" only to discover that the person is not a leader of people so much as she is a well-known or popular individual. Mary Higgins Clark sells millions of novels, but that does not make her a leader in the field of fiction writing. Glen Rice scores a lot of points for the Knicks, but that does not make him the team leader.

THE HEART OF LEADERSHIP

Leadership is more than calling the shots, and it is more than merely having influence on people's thoughts and behavior. Similarly, holding a position or title that implies a person is a leader bears little relationship to whether, in reality, the person is a leader. Neither does possessing a charismatic personality or massive intellect make a person a leader.

A leader succeeds only if
his or her followers succeed.

Leadership is about calling, character, and competencies—a complete package of components that enables a leader to help people reach their goals and potential. By focusing on the will of God and the needs of His creation, a leader is ultimately a servant. It is only by encouraging, empowering, enforcing, and evaluating that a leader assists people in their quest to achieve meaning and fulfillment in life. In other words, a leader succeeds only if his or her followers succeed, and the followers succeed only if their leader is sensitive and responsive to God and empowers the people to do His will.

To lead people means that you motivate, mobilize, direct, and resource them so that they are able to fulfill a vision that they have agreed is appropriate and worthy of their pursuit.[1] But perhaps the definition of leadership raises a question in your mind: Who can do all of that with excellence, especially in a broad and complicated environment?

Let me broach the topic from a different angle. One of the most common complaints I hear from pastors is that they want lay-people to be involved as leaders in ministry, but they simply cannot find enough qualified and competent people to fill the various leadership posts within their ministry. Frankly, if they are seeking a score of dynamic, charismatic, articulate, multitalented, universally loved individuals who will provide outstanding direction and support to church people, always know what to say, can solve everyone's problems, create efficient procedures, and consistently develop creative strategies and plans, then they are right: We do not have enough of those people to get the job done.

God, however, never sets us up for failure; He always provides His people with whatever resources they need—and when they need them—to accomplish His will. The fact that churches do not have a plentiful source of high-powered, intelligent, aggressive, supercompetent, highly regarded, productive leaders is not because God has forgotten what we need to faithfully and effectively serve Him. God never intended for any church to have an abundance of such people, because He never intended for us to desert one of the most significant leadership models that He provided for us—that is, the model of team leadership.

REDEFINING MINISTRY LEADERSHIP

In my research with churches across the nation, I have recognized two realities: First, quality leadership is indispensable to ministry success (defined as consistent and widespread life transformation), and second, we expect too much of individual leaders.

In other words, what may seem like a contradiction (that is, that God expects leaders to facilitate the pursuit and fulfillment of the vision He gives them, but He does not provide many individuals with extraordinary leadership capabilities) is not really a contradiction at all. The problem is *not* that we do not have enough good leaders, but that we have an errant expectation about what a leader is called to do.

Had the church relied upon a single, incredibly gifted, magnetic individual to replace Jesus, the church would surely have collapsed.

With characteristic grace and wisdom, God has provided us with all the resources we need to accomplish His ends on earth. He has even provided us with the leadership talent pool that we may draw from—if we know what we're looking for. If you think about Jesus' disciples, it doesn't take long to realize that few of them seemed like the strong, visionary, world-changing leader we seek in a senior pastor today. Instead, Jesus used gifted, capable individuals who simply needed training and vision.

The story of the church, as depicted in the book of Acts, is one of a community of faith directed by a team of leaders working together toward a common vision. Had the church relied upon a single, incredibly gifted, magnetic individual to replace Jesus, the church would surely have collapsed. What the disciples discovered was that none of them had the complete package of gifts, abilities, and insights necessary to facilitate the growth of the Christian church, but each had a very significant and defined role to play in that revolutionary undertaking.

We often think of our age and our tools as the most sophisticated in human history. Perhaps that is true. But one other reality is also true: "There is nothing new under the sun" (Ecclesiastes 1:9). Throughout history, people have benefited from having teams of leaders that provided the direction they needed. We may read stories about individual leaders who were unusually gifted and capable, but those people are the exception to the rule. Much of the great leadership delivered throughout the ages has come from teams, even if the public's sense of that guidance was largely related to one person's performance.

Is your church led by a "superstar" leader or by a leadership team?

What Is a Leadership Team?

Most churches employ two types of gatherings for productive purposes: work groups and committees. *Work groups* are collections of people who come together for a particular duration to accomplish a specific task. The task is not necessarily vision-driven, and the group's focus might not be the future. A work group generally does not have the special combination of spiritual gifts and natural talents required to accomplish the plethora of outcomes that move the church toward the fulfillment of God's vision. A *committee* is a collection of individuals who meet for discussion and perhaps to make recommendations regarding policy, programs, or plans. Committees typically have little, if any, authority to act. Often they provide the organization with ideas, preferences, or suggestions that a leadership body then considers and passes judgment upon.

A *leadership team* is quite different. It is a small group of leaders who possess complementary gifts and skills. They are committed to one another's growth and success and hold themselves mutually accountable. Together they lead a larger group of people toward a common vision, specific performance goals, and a plan of action.

That definition of effective leadership teams combines seven key components worthy of further exploration:

1. *Small group.* A large group cannot lead. Anyone who has been involved in effective leadership knows that once a team gets beyond six people, it becomes unwieldy and degenerates into compromises that reflect the lowest common denominator. At that stage, the focus of the group is not upon a commonly held vision but upon producing some tangible outcome with which everyone is comfortable. That is not leadership, it is accommodation. Effective leadership teams typically have three to five people. Less than three leaves you without the horsepower to get the job done. More than five produces inefficiencies and excessive compromise.

2. *Leaders.* A leadership team is a collection of leaders—not warm bodies willing to help out, not people with titles,

but individuals who possess the calling, character, and competencies that qualify them as leaders. Since the very purpose of the team is to provide leadership, it must contain individuals who have that capability. Further, the notion of leaders implies that there are also followers. A leadership team is of no significance unless it is helping followers to understand, adopt, and accomplish a common vision.

3. *Complementary gifts and skills.* One of the most important attributes of effective leadership teams is that the leaders have a combination of gifts and skills that complement one another. One of the worst imaginable scenarios is to have three or four people with identical gifts and talents working in a team: You will experience tension and conflict of world-class proportions! A team is effective when four specific leadership aptitudes are fully and broadly represented among the team members. (We will discuss these leadership aptitudes in chapter 6.)

4. *Committed to one another.* In a true team, the leaders are committed to one another's growth and success in ministry. Granted, these individuals may not become best friends, but they must respect one another and care about their colleagues' personal maturation. Unless team members experience such ongoing growth, the team will

suffer. Because a team is an expression of community, mutual concern is an indispensable ingredient in the team dynamic. A team in which the members are not committed to one another is a team that may produce some desirable results, but it is not likely to achieve its full potential as a team.

5. *Common vision.* It is the corporate vision that brings the team together and facilitates its passion to move forward as one. The vision unites and excites those who wish to be part of the process. The vision serves as the filter through which efforts are examined and success is defined by progress made toward fulfilling the vision. The vision is the core concept that the team communicates to the population it is leading. Not only must the leadership team be united in its acceptance of and devotion to the vision, but unless the team can inspire others to own the vision, the team will fail in its efforts.

6. *Goals and plan.* A vision that has no goals and plans associated with it is merely a fantasy. A team without goals and plans is merely a social club. Leaders must move toward the vision by identifying realistic and mea-surable goals before they can facilitate the development of specific courses of action that will produce the required outcomes.

7. *Mutually accountable.* One of the distinctives of leadership teams is their determination to evaluate their own efforts and enable one another to live up to specific standards—both team standards and individual standards. One reason leaders fall into disgrace is that they do not have people who know them and whom they trust to bring them into accountability. Great teams are comprised of leaders who have developed sufficient trust, rapport, and vulnerability to keep one another honest, focused, productive, humble, and inspired.

When these elements are combined, the result is a powerful assembly of individuals whose ability to serve others is multiplied beyond what any one could accomplish alone. Yes, teams sometimes make mistakes, lose their way, or fall victim to intrateam conflicts. But more often than not, leaders love working in teams and are ecstatic about the outcomes of the team's efforts.

TEAM LEADERSHIP IN THE LARGE CHURCH

Less than 2 percent of America's Protestant churches attracts one thousand or more adults each weekend; less than one of every seven has attendance exceeding six hundred in a typical week. But despite their relative scarcity in the church landscape, large churches have enormous influence in the church marketplace. Having reached a different scale of ministry, are large churches exempt from the necessity of utilizing team leadership?

Our study found just the opposite: A large church that does not use teams will suffer. Specifically, its leaders will be burned out, the church's capacity to minister effectively will be limited, its senior pastor will become either a cult hero or a blockage to the ministry process, and the ministry will become less participative. The larger a church gets, the more imperative it becomes for its leaders to minister within a team culture instead of as solo practitioners. Not only is the ministry output more significant when a staff works as a team, but their cooperative effort also models true teamwork for the laity. The result is greater ministry satisfaction among the clergy, a better learning process for lay leaders, and heightened transformational capacity.

TEAM LEADERSHIP IN THE SMALL CHURCH

While most pastors aspire to lead large churches, the reality is that the majority of American churches has fewer than one hundred adults attending on any given weekend. Less than one in five churches has more than one full-time professional on the church payroll. In other words, most churches are the equivalent of a sole proprietorship (a "soul" pastorship, maybe?) that might appear to preclude such churches from utilizing the pastor in team leadership. Indeed, the fact that a huge majority of churches does not have more than one or two ministry professionals on the payroll emphasizes two important conditions: the necessity of laity involvement in leadership and the significance of teams as the leadership framework.

Once again our research shows that not only can teams work in a small church environment, but that the better they work, the more likely it is that the church will not remain small for long. When leaders combine their efforts with those of others who possess complementary gifts, that mixture is likely to boost the impact of the church within the community and attract many curious people—some of whom will be impressed enough to stay and add their efforts to the ministry mix. As in any other scenario, the pastor must lead the way, but he or she must do so by being a team player—a leader of leaders, certainly, but also a colleague in ministry serving in harmony with the contingent of leaders God has brought to the church.

CONSUMING MINISTRY OR DOING MINISTRY?

Those who criticize the church for the consumer mentality of Christians often miss the boat, not because they find fault with the consumption of religious resources by churchgoers, but because they fail to take their complaints deep enough to understand the roots of the problem. Many churchgoers have no choice but to *consume* ministry because they are not invited and prepared to *do* ministry. The desire to somehow engage in spiritual activity moves millions of individuals, many of whom may indeed be gifted as potential leaders, to settle for watching ministry rather than engaging in ministry. The passive observation of ministry is often a result of pastors who reject the possibilities afforded by team leadership. Instead, tens of thousands of pastors "protect" the church's ministry by waiting for the "right" person to come along who can provide compelling, irresistible, multifaceted leadership. Of course, such a person rarely comes along, leaving the church dissipated by missed opportunities, dashed hopes, and depressed progress.

> *Many churchgoers have no choice but to consume ministry because they are not invited and prepared to do ministry.*

In the meantime, by excluding lay leaders from exercising their gifts, the church becomes just another example of professional service delivery: trained and certified professionals (clergy) providing the goods and services (worship events, classes) needed or desired by consumers (congregants). The ministry's potential is therefore limited by the capacity of the professionals on the payroll.

Rejecting team leadership essentially ignores biblical precedent and principles. Believers are entrusted with special abilities (that is, spiritual gifts) so that they may serve God and His people more effectively. Preventing people from using their spiritual gifts diminishes the joy of ministry and reduces the health of the church. Conversely, identifying just a handful of leadership superstars to carry the church sets up those individuals for failure and frustration. In fact, by emphasizing solo leadership, we inadvertently focus on what we accomplish based on our unique talents and stellar efforts, rather than upon God and what He is able to accomplish through us via the empowerment of His Holy Spirit. Ministry leadership is not the exclusive domain of clergy but a discipline to be practiced by all those whom God has called and equipped for the function of leading the church. If effective leadership is going to take place in our churches, it will be largely because laypeople are using their leadership abilities.

THE BIBLE AND TEAMS

I sometimes cringe when I read an impassioned plea for Christians or churches to adopt a particular perspective or practice because it is biblical, only to find the scriptural evidence to be forced. Let me be forthright about the role of teams in the Bible: God's Word does not make a big deal about the importance of leaders serving in teams. Most of the wisdom gleaned regarding teams must be drawn from passages or stories in which the key principles relate to other aspects of life and ministry. In fact, while I believe the Bible is a great text on leadership, it directly discusses leadership in relatively few passages; most leadership principles derived from the Bible are inferential. With this caveat in mind, let me suggest a few ways in which the Bible endorses the value and significance of team-based leadership.

Moses

Moses was a fascinating leader. Reluctant to lead from the start, he learned many leadership lessons the hard way. Two insights stand out about Moses and his involvement with teams. First, he clearly recognized that while God called him to lead, he was hampered by severe limitations and was reticent to take on such responsibility. His reaction was to ask God to provide him with colleagues who could compensate for his overt weaknesses—that is, to let him lead as part of a team in which he would (by God's design) serve as the directing leader and captain of the team. In response, God provided other leaders, such as Joshua and Caleb, to share the burden.

Solo leadership can take you only as far as your individual capacity.

The second insight relates to the potential inefficiencies of solo leadership. Even though Moses had capable teammates, he retained much of the responsibility for directing the people, making public policy, and supervising the operations of their venture. In Exodus 18, Moses' father-in-law, Jethro, pays Moses and his family a visit. He observes Moses' typical workday and is appalled by the bottleneck Moses has created by striving to be all things to all people. Jethro offers some simple advice: Divide the leadership duties into manageable portions and delegate some of the responsibility to a leadership team of other gifted servants. That advice changed Moses' life, freeing him to focus on aspects of directing the nation that only he could perform. Solo leadership can take you only as far as your individual capacity; increasing the leadership capacity through teamwork enhances the quality of life for the people as well as for you, their leader.

Nehemiah

Throughout his campaign to restore the city walls, Nehemiah relied heavily upon teams of gifted individuals with complementary skills to facilitate the fulfillment of the vision God had given to him. At different times throughout the campaign he organized different teams for divergent purposes. The walls would never have been built if he had relied upon a more traditional style of one-man leadership.

Jesus

Doesn't it seem most sensible that to accomplish a spiritual end, Jesus would have turned to the people most interested in spirituality—the religious leaders of the day? And wouldn't you expect Him, given barely three years in public ministry, to pursue alliances with high-profile individuals whose résumés proved that they knew how to lead effectively? But, as usual, Jesus broke all the rules. He called upon a group of uneducated, low-key, ill-trained individuals whose character seemed pretty solid and who were willing to sacrifice whatever they had to in order to be apprentices to the master leader. Clearly, Jesus' intent was not to raise up eleven future hotshots whose stellar performances would wow the world, but rather to prepare a humble group whose limitations would force them to work together to complete the assignment He had given them while remaining focused on Him. Jesus was training teams of leaders, not potential members of the Future CEO Club.

Paul

On his missionary journeys the most prolific of the apostles always traveled and ministered with a team. Whether it was in the company of Barnabas, John, Simeon, Lucius, or Manaen (Acts 13), serving with Timothy, Judas, or Silas (Acts 15–16), or ministering alongside various combinations of other leaders, Paul was the quintessential team player. His advice in Ephesians 4:12, "to prepare God's people for works of service, so that the body of Christ may be built up," remains one of the central challenges to the church to train laity to do the entire work of the ministry. His entries regarding spiritual gifts (1 Corinthians 12 and Romans 12) not only identify leadership as a core gift, but further suggest that rather than focus on one individual who can do it all, God's intent was to prepare each of us to be a role player, not a superhero.

ONLY ONE MINISTRY SUPERSTAR

There are other Bible passages in both the Old and New Testaments that address the importance of leadership provided through teams of gifted individuals. The point is not to diminish the value of individual leaders but simply to recognize that the Bible does acknowledge teams as a viable leadership strategy.

My passion is for God's leaders to express their leadership calling, character, and competencies within the optimal environment for the advancement of His kingdom. In some situations this will mean solo leadership; in others, the optimal approach is to lead in a team-based environment. The longer we deny the benefits of team leadership, the less likely it is that we will experience the power of God in the church, in society, or in our personal efforts.

There is only one ministry superstar: Jesus Christ. If we persist in seeking to lead churches through the display of talents and abilities resident within only a few unusually capable individuals, rather than allowing the community of believers to use their significant-but-less-inclusive leadership skills in an orchestrated unison to accomplish synergistic outcomes, the church and society will pay the price for such defiance.

CHAPTER THREE

WITHOUT VISION, THERE IS NO LEADERSHIP

---

*God has a unique vision
for your church and a significant vision
for each ministry within your church.*

Vision is to a leader as air is to a human being: Without it, you die.

To be effective, the leaders of a church must have a clear and motivating grasp of God's vision for their ministry. Likewise, the leaders working together in a team must possess a firm understanding of God's vision for the team as it fits within the encompassing vision of the church in which they serve.

The concept of vision is thousands of years old. It has shaped cultures for centuries and has touched the lives of people on every continent. Consider some of the historical statements about vision.

God inspired Solomon to write concerning the centrality of vision, "Where there is no vision, the people perish" (Proverbs

29:18, KJV). *The New International Version* translates the passage as "Where there is no revelation, the people cast off restraint." My favorite interpretation of this verse is from *The Living Bible:* "Where there is ignorance of God, the people run wild." Vision comes from God Himself to keep His people focused, under control, and devoted to endeavors that are meaningful to them and Him.

An ancient Chinese proverb admonishes people to devote themselves to what is most important and to discern that by thinking circumspectly about the future: "If your vision is for one year, plant wheat. If your vision is for a decade, plant trees. If your vision is for a lifetime, plant people." Ideally, vision is not for the short term.

Great artists are people of vision; through their art they create something beautiful or meaningful out of nothing. The renowned Italian artist Michelangelo prayed that God would keep his vision alive. "Lord, grant that I may always desire to do more than I am able to accomplish." Vision, the concept of what does not exist but could, is what motivates us to continue to strive toward the fulfillment of that outcome.

Pastor and civil rights activist Martin Luther King Jr. challenged his followers to commit themselves to a worthy vision. "If a man hasn't discovered something he will die for, he isn't fit to live." That "something" alluded to by King was God's vision. For him, it was a world in which racial discrimination was nowhere to be found, where love reigned supreme and overcame all distinctions and inequalities based on race, creed, or background.

God has a unique vision for your church and a significant

vision for each ministry within your church. He provides this vision to His called, gifted leaders for the purpose of strategically directing the resources of the church. Grasping, casting, and indefatigably pursuing God's vision is the central, defining characteristic of God's leaders. It is the commitment to that vision, and our capacity to bring it to fruition, that dictates the shape of the church and the depth of influence that the church has on the world.

Why is vision so critical to leadership? Simply put, if you cannot articulate a clear picture of what you are seeking to achieve, how can you lead people there? Since a leader must motivate, mobilize, and direct people, on what basis would you accomplish such outcomes without casting a compelling vision? At the most basic level, realize that a leader is taking people somewhere. Without vision, where would you lead them?

> *If you cannot articulate a clear picture of what you*
> *are seeking to achieve, how can you lead people there?*

Therein lies one of the secrets to why churches are not having the impact they could. Great leadership lies at the heart of every successful ministry, and vision is at the heart of great leadership. Many churches struggle either because they are headed by people who aren't leaders or they have otherwise-capable leaders who do not possess God's vision for their ministry.[1]

Without leaders who hold a firm understanding of God's vision, the entire church suffers.

- Vision inspires people by providing them with hope, meaning, and significant challenges; the absence of vision robs them of inspiration.

- Vision attracts people to a cause by giving them something worth investing in and something to focus on that transcends the mundane endeavors of daily life; the absence of vision relegates them to a life of insignificance and disengagement from things that have eternal meaning.

- Vision builds community by providing people with a common purpose and putting their natural competitiveness and pettiness in perspective; the absence of vision prevents them from building life-changing relationships and from diminishing the tendency to see the worst in others.

- Vision sustains people by giving them a compelling reason to persevere and to stay focused on what really matters; the absence of vision facilitates majoring on the minors.

PERSPECTIVE IN MINISTRY

Three significant concepts govern the nature and perspective of your ministry: mission, vision, and values. How do they work together in a church?[2]

Mission describes your overall purpose for existence. When you describe your mission to someone, you define the most fundamental understanding of what you are striving to accomplish. The mission of a church is to facilitate meaningful worship, evangelism, discipleship, service, stewardship, and fellowship—or, more succinctly, to facilitate life transformation through which people become evermore like Jesus Christ. The mission of an evangelist is to win souls to Christ. The mission of a leader is to motivate, mobilize, resource, and direct people to fulfill a vision.

Every Christian church has the same mission as every other Christian church. Every Christian evangelist has the same mission as every other Christian evangelist. Every leader in Christian ministry has the same mission as every other leader in Christian ministry. They exist to see similar outcomes happen, and yet each ministry is unique and is not interchangeable with the other. That's where vision comes into the picture.

Vision is focused guidance that helps you determine the unique way in which you have been called to fulfill the mission. Mission without vision leads to frustration and paralysis because it can never be completed or perfectly fulfilled—it is too general and too broad. Mission, while vital, is too generic to point you in a specific direction; vision is the idiosyncratic way in which God wants to use you to complete a part of the grand puzzle of the development of His kingdom. Vision tells you what you should do, in specific ways, to produce results that honor God by fulfilling the special role He has carved out for you.

Values play an important role in this process too. Values are the principles and standards that define what is right, desirable, and worthwhile. Values relate to character as experienced through a person's thoughts, words, and behaviors. The values you possess constitute the nonnegotiable outcomes of your being—the ways of living that are acceptable, appropriate, and desirable from your frame of reference. Every individual lives in accordance with personal values, whether they have been articulated or not. In the same way, every church operates in concert with its values, whether they are clearly defined or latent.

Working together, mission is about participating in the purposes of God's kingdom. Vision distills your unique, small-but-necessary role in doing so. And values provide the behavioral parameters that limit what you may and may not do in the process of pursuing the vision. These three notions, blended into a coherent concept of reality, provide the directing perspective for your church or your life. Every church must clearly identify its mission, vision, and values so that people understand what it stands for, where it is going, and what is permissible in the process. Similarly, every Christian individual should identify his or her mission, vision, and values for life and ministry and use those insights to determine why to live, how to live, and where to minister. And, of course, every leader and leadership team must be able to articulate God's mission, vision, and values for the leader and for the team, providing a clear sense of how to make life and ministry glorifying to God, beneficial to the church, and personally meaningful and fulfilling.

DEFINING VISION MORE SPECIFICALLY

As you strive to understand God's vision for your church, your life, or your team, think of it as *a compelling mental portrait of a preferable future* communicated by God to His chosen leaders and based upon an accurate understanding of God, self, and circumstances.

God's vision, whether it is for the organization, the individual, or a team of individuals serving the organization, is irresistible to those who have been called to partake in its pursuit. It is so personally exciting that it stimulates a deep desire to be involved in making it real. The concept itself is so real that you can see it clearly in your mind, just like a portrait painted for you by a renowned artist. The vision will be both exciting and unnerving, since it inevitably calls for change—but change from what exists to something indisputably superior. God's vision always builds a bridge from the past to the future.

He relies upon His chosen leaders to seek, grasp, communicate, and pursue His vision with vigor and diligence. That vision is the strategic fulfillment of the mission, but it must be operationalized if it is to be of any worth. This is accomplished by converting the concept of a preferable reality into a series of *specific goals* (measurable outcomes that relate to the mission, vision, and values), *strategies* (general approaches designed to facilitate the accomplishment of the specified goals), and *tactics* (specific actions that relate to the strategies undertaken to achieve specific goals).

Can you see the interrelatedness of these elements—and the

distinctiveness of each? A ministry or team that operates solely on the basis of *mission* won't get very far because it has no real sense of direction; thus it will see limited impact and lack the passion to sustain its efforts over time. A ministry or team that has never delineated its *values* will get into trouble because any behavior can be justified by results—a philosophy antithetical to biblical Christianity. A ministry or team that strives to implement a *vision* without understanding the larger framework within which it fits and without a connection to specified values will be a task-oriented ministry that misses the mark.[3]

DISCERNING YOUR CHURCH'S VISION

If you have been called to lead others for the purposes of His kingdom, the vision God gives you will become the centerpiece of your ministry. It will be the basis against which your ministry efforts should be judged, your motivation for continuing in the face of daunting challenges, and the foundation of your attempts to enlist others in fulfilling the vision.

Because that vision is the core of what you relate to as a leader or as a team, discerning God's vision is one of the first tasks a leader or team should address. Focusing on His vision will bring you closer to Him, give you strength and clarity regarding your life, increase your leadership influence, build your confidence in your ability to make good decisions, keep you encouraged during tough times, release you from the oppressive tyranny of making choices on the basis of feelings and politics, and enable you to eliminate distractions and diversions from your life without feeling guilty. Leaders pay a price for the privilege of leading God's people—just look at what Jesus, Moses, Paul, and Peter went through as they sought to be faithful to God's vision for their lives. But keep in mind that your personal investment in carrying out God's vision will pay off many times over the course of your ministry. (Several thousand years of recorded history among the people of God support that claim.)

> *Discerning God's vision is one of the first tasks
> a leader or team should address.*

Perhaps you're asking a very basic question at this point: How do you attain God's vision? After years of study on this topic, including evaluations of how many of our most effective ministry leaders have arrived at a clarity regarding God's vision for them, it seems that the process itself is quite simple. I believe there are four steps involved.

1. Know Yourself Inside Out

That means understanding your personal strengths and weaknesses, your joys and fears, your past successes and failures, your character flaws, the spiritual gifts God has entrusted to you, your natural skills and abilities, and so on. All of these elements ultimately relate to who you are, how you relate to God, how He can use you, and what you must do to become the type of individual He can rely upon to do great things for His kingdom. You cannot be effective—or trusted—until you know yourself, because deep-rooted change will not occur until an honest self-examination and personal spiritual enhancement process has been undertaken. God does not seek perfect people as leaders, but He does want people who are committed to serving Him as best they can. This self-assessment effort is critical to God's being able to trust you with a vision of how and where to lead His people.

2. Know Your Ministry Environment and the Related Opportunities

Naturally, you should have a firm understanding of the nature of your church—its mission, vision, and values, along with the resident spiritual gifts, natural talents, physical resources, ministry opportunities, congregational history, and the like. You also need to know your community—its prevailing values, most-widespread felt needs, and people's life expectations. Make it a priority to become intimately acquainted with your ministry colleagues in the area—their mission, vision, and values as well as their key programs, successes and failures, priorities, and capabilities.

3. Know God

Of course, it is critical to have a deep, robust relationship with God through prayer, worship, and meditation on His Word and principles—spiritual disciplines that enable you to supernaturally connect with the living God. Beyond that, you must understand how He works—the nature of His character, how He interacts with leaders, and the expectations He has for them. You can glean many such insights from studying the Bible. These efforts will help you sharpen your focus on Him and draw you closer, which then facilitates an understanding of what He is calling you to pursue.

Once you have committed to the process of discerning the vision, it will take time to grasp the ministry concept God has designed for you. Through a diligent regimen of prayer, reflection, Scripture study, examining your ministry context, and exploring the wisdom of trusted believers who know you and your ministry well, chances are good that the vision will be incrementally revealed to you. But before you run with it, there is one more crucial step to take.

4. Test the Vision

Test the vision you feel God is giving you by obtaining feedback from the handful of intimate counselors you trust, by evaluating the opened doors for ministry that coincide with your view of the vision, and by taking a step of faith to see what happens as you launch out toward fulfilling the vision. This will help you be certain that you have God's vision before you choose to broadcast that declaration to others.

NOT A MATTER OF CONSENSUS

In the discernment process, keep in mind that *vision is not the result of consensus.* What God wants does not rely upon a majority vote or some other democratic process. Man's ways are not God's ways, and we must be prepared to accept God's vision even if it seems at odds with human wisdom. Committees, study commissions, denominational entities, and congregations are not the means through which God delivers His vision to a leader. Instead, God goes direct. This underscores why the capacity to understand and remain focused upon vision is one of the hallmarks of a leader.

God's vision often calls for us to achieve things we cannot achieve by human means. And that is His intent. If it were outcomes that we could accomplish without reliance upon Him, then the vision would defeat His desire to be in living partnership with us. Neither is His vision for us ever related or limited to numerical growth. He desires growth in character, exhibited through radical obedience and absolute commitment, regardless of how many people accept that challenge. The vision will be more specific than just devouring the Word, seeking souls, or worshiping Him—we're all called to do such basic acts of homage—and it will take more than just a few years to accomplish. Vision is for the long term, and it will probably take you a substantial period of time—months, perhaps even a year or two—to determine the vision.

> *God's vision often calls for us to achieve things*
> *we cannot achieve by human means.*

Within the team context, realize that we are dealing with individual leaders, each of whom will have a personal vision from God for his or her life and ministry. Successful teams are those that bring together leaders driven by compatible visions. For instance, you might search for leaders who have vision related to discipleship. Let them discuss among themselves how they could work together to lead the church forward into a more effective and dynamic discipling ministry. Lay leaders whose passion is worship might find that their personal vision coincides perfectly with the vision God entrusted to other leaders in the church regarding the ministry of worship. What emerges for the worship leadership team, then, is likely the result of a handful of leaders who share a passion for worship and find common ground in the vision with which God has empowered each of them.

GETTING THE RIGHT VISION

A key point that has not yet been sufficiently emphasized is that the emergent vision must be God's, not ours. The tendency is for leaders to evaluate their resources and opportunities and develop a vision based on their own inclinations—which often gets the church into trouble. Consider the differences between our vision and that provided to us by God.

For starters, human vision is quite limiting. We base our vision on what we can accomplish when we maximize our natural talents and skills. God's vision, however, pushes us beyond our capacity to achieve things that can only be ascribed to the work of the supernatural. God is not interested in what we can do; He is interested in what He can do through us when we are willing vessels.

Typically, human vision is determined by that which brings us delight. After surveying the possibilities, we lean toward those outcomes that we find most appealing, exhilarating, or exciting. The reason to pursue God's vision, though, is that it is His vision that brings Him the greatest delight. Our grandest ideas pale in comparison to His plans for us. If we are truly in tune with Him, then doing whatever brings honor, glory, and pleasure to God is what makes our life worth living.

Often, human vision is dangerous because it is ego-driven. But when we strive to understand and pursue God's vision, we exhibit a satisfying degree of obedience, submission, and humility. Our vision may be something to which we could commit, but His vision is something over which we should obsess.

Do not reject a vision because it isn't what you were hoping for. If it is truly God's vision, it is perfect, and He will bless you as you seek to fulfill it. Do not assume it is not His vision for you simply because it is uncomfortable. Whenever you devote yourself to obeying God, you declare yourself an enemy of Satan and of the world—and you'd better expect opposition and suffering. Great Christian leaders enter the battlefield aware of the challenge they face, prepared to fight the good fight rather than seek the easy path. Just as the apostle Paul had to suffer many things for the sake of Christ, the more responsible we become in the Lord's army, the weightier the challenges we can expect to face. Faith in God and continued joy in being able to serve Him as leaders will move us beyond anything we might otherwise have achieved in life.

MAXIMIZING THE VISION

To make the most of the vision that God reveals to you, protect it and convey it to those who will partner with you in pursuing it.

Initially, thank God for allowing you to receive the vision and for the incredible responsibility and trust He has extended to you as a leader who has been given such vision. It is His gift to you— a tool to facilitate effective leadership, significant ministry and life meaning, and transformation for many. Own that vision as dearly as anything in your life, allowing yourself to be both humbled and energized by it. Pray constantly that God will bless you as you pursue it, and never fail to give Him the glory as aspects of the vision become reality. Commit yourself to faithfully and endlessly carry out that challenge.

In the process, remember that you are now the champion of the vision. You must protect it from being dissipated, ignored, and carried out halfheartedly. One of your key roles, then, is to spread and nurture the vision. You must use whatever means are at your disposal to communicate the vision to those who will play a part in its life. That demands that you write the vision in a comprehensive fashion—an exhaustive documentation of the vision, as you understand it, in its totality. You'll also want to write a vision statement—a brief summary of the heart of the vision, captured in fifteen to twenty-five words that are descriptive, precise, and inspiring—identifying the action that is required. Raise the vision during meetings and discussions and relate decisions back to the vision. Evaluate outcomes in light of the vision. Hire staff in relation to their acceptance and passion regarding the vision of the ministry unit with which they will most commonly interface. Never let people forget the vision; that is a leader's responsibility.

Keeping the vision alive is critical, but striving to strategically accomplish it is the bottom line for church leaders. Unless you act on it, vision is just a dream—interesting but ultimately worthless. Failure to implement the vision is a rejection of God's gift to you and of His plan for His people. Faithfully executing strategies and tactics that make His vision real will bring purpose, joy, and influence into your life and that of the church.

CHURCH VISION VS. TEAM VISION

Now let's clarify the relationship between the vision of the church, the vision of the team, and the vision of the individual leader.

From a leadership vantage point, a church operates at two levels: the aggregate (congregational) level and the component ministry level. The *aggregate level* encompasses everything the church does. It is a core obligation of the senior pastor, as the primary, God-ordained leader of the church, to identify and articulate that corporate vision for the congregation. The pastor must not simply impose his or her vision for the church on the congregation, but he or she must listen to God and discern what He has in mind for the church. The pastor then communicates God's vision for the church's comprehensive ministry to the body of members. Everything that takes place at the church from that point forward must be filtered through the simple question: Does this proposed activity or policy support our vision? In essence, this church vision statement is an umbrella vision, and all activity within the church must be considered in light of the church's vision no matter what the component ministry focus might be.

The pastor alone cannot make the vision happen; he or she will work with a team of leaders at the corporate level to ensure that the church stays on target. That corporate-level leadership team, perhaps comprised of the senior pastor and a handful of elders or other key lay leaders, is responsible for making sure that the vision is known, understood, owned, and pursued by the congregation.

> *The pastor alone cannot*
> *make the vision happen.*

At the same time, that aggregate vision will become real through the work of various *component ministries* within the church such as worship, evangelism, discipleship, stewardship, community service, and congregational community. In other words, the corporate vision is made real through teams of leaders whose efforts are blessed by the corporate leadership team in order to orchestrate the church's ministry development and vision fulfillment. Each of the component ministries will identify its own vision statement for its area of focus and will pursue its vision by developing goals, strategies, and tactics designed to facilitate the ministry and spiritual maturing of congregants. The component ministry will have its own team to articulate its vision, develop its plans, lead work groups and ancillary teams in carrying out its vision, and interact with the corporate leadership team to coordinate all ministry efforts. In so doing, each component ministry vision will help facilitate the achievement of the church's macro-level vision.

When a ministry team strives to determine its vision, it will have two primary constraints. First, its team vision must fit snuggly within the contours and confines of the church's aggregate ministry. Second, the team's ministry will result from a combining of the personal visions of the team members—individuals who share a common passion for involvement in and leadership of that component of ministry. These individuals bring their individual visions to the team for consideration of what God wants to do among them.

THE SAGA OF FIRST BAPTIST CHURCH

Here is an example of how the process works. James Barton was called as pastor of First Baptist Church eleven years ago.[4] Located in the Midwest, the church owned its small but tidy facility in a valley of mixed industrial and agricultural businesses populated mostly by middle-class and blue-collar families. The church had about three hundred adults attending on a regular basis, plus eighty-some children and teens who participated in the youth program. Shortly after Barton's arrival, it became clear to him that, while the church conducted lots of ministry activity, the efforts were not related to a grand vision of what God wanted First Baptist to accomplish. The church was simply doing its best to do what churches do—provide a worship service and Christian education program every Sunday, a family service Sunday night, a youth program on Wednesdays, and a parcel of other ministries (women's, men's, soup kitchen, etc.) whenever those groups were able to do something.

Pastor Barton spent about four months getting to know the people of First Baptist and becoming familiar with the other ministers and churches in town. He spent time gathering facts about the community and its population, as well as delving into the history of the church. After this period of "doing my homework," Pastor Barton began meeting with key congregants to ask their support in what he described as "the most important chapter in the church's seventy-year history: seeking God's vision for the church." He was able to enlist several dozen leaders and other church members into praying for him and with him to prepare for a new era in the church's life.

Another seven months went by before Pastor Barton felt that he had truly heard from God regarding why He wanted First Baptist to continue and how First Baptist could benefit the kingdom. The pastor spent another month carefully describing the outlines of vision to key leaders and church members, seeking their input and reshaping the vision around their ideas. The heart of the vision did not change, but the ways in which he began to convey the vision reflected some of the insights, experiences, passions, and sensitivities of his congregants. Eventually, after minor revisions to the church values statement, the pastor crafted the following mission and vision statements:

> **Our Mission:** To love God and His creation
> through a biblical ministry of worship, discipleship,
> evangelism, and service.

Our Vision: To promote constant and genuine worship in multiple forms and venues throughout the valley, to strengthen believers and transform nonbelievers.

Pastor Barton spent the next quarter attempting to break down the vision into a palatable perspective for all who called First Baptist their church home. His deliberations had persuaded him that God was calling First Baptist, which had an outstanding worship ministry and a glut of capable musicians, to become the premiere worship ministry in the area. More important, though, Barton was struck by the notion that worship was to be the church's means of impacting people's lives—fortifying the spiritual strength of congregants through a deep and intense experience with God and His Word as well as exposing nonbelievers to the presence of God through worship. The vision called for the church to base all of its ministry endeavors, both on and off the church's modest campus, on riveting worship. That meant offering to provide worship segments at local conferences and public meetings and offering to help other churches with their worship ministries. This was a big step for First Baptist. It had never been publicly known for its worship, but now its primary thrust would focus on how authentic, intense worship could transform saints and sinners alike.

To get this vision across to the people in the congregation, the pastor spent that three-month period preaching, teaching, meeting, speaking, and writing articles for church publications regarding the meaning and implications of the vision statement. He had two or three one-to-one meetings almost four days each week for a month, meeting with the church's most influential members to lay out in detail the implications of the vision for the church and for the individual with whom he was meeting. He also spent time interacting with area pastors to inform them of the new developments and initiate conversations as to how First Baptist might be able to minister more cooperatively with other churches.

Finally, after three months of such preparation, he gained the enthusiastic endorsement of the mission and vision statements by the existing lay leaders and then by the entire congregation.

His next task was to align the church's organizational structure with the vision and with some of the initial goals he set for the church in response to the vision statement. Having come from a team-based ministry in his prior church, Pastor Barton was determined to transform First Baptist into a church led by lay teams. He conceived a transition process with the following phases:

1. Communicate the concept.

2. Gain individual and committee support.

3. Identify a pilot team and lay leaders.

4. Invite those leaders to participate in specific ministry leadership teams.

5. Provide leadership training.

6. Institute an organizational transition process for the church.

7. Release the teams to lead.

That process, which encountered some serious obstacles when a group of long-term elders resisted being reassigned to different positions, took slightly more than two years to put into effect.

> *After overcoming the typical discomforts and struggles, the team began to appreciate its diversity and breadth of capacity.*

By the time the transition was completed, Pastor Barton was working smoothly with the Executive Ministry Team (EMT) of First Baptist. That team consisted of the pastor, who was a directing leader; two elders, one a strategic leader and the other an operational leader; and an additional layman, a gifted team-building leader. (While the church did not use those titles for their leaders, they were cognizant of the diverse leadership gifts and skills each brought to the process and came to appreciate the synergistic results.) After overcoming the typical discomforts and struggles of a newly formed team—such as not always accepting the ideas of the pastor, striving to understand the perspective of colleagues from different emotional or intellectual starting points, and interpreting the vision differently in relation to various opportunities or challenges—the team began to appreciate its diversity and breadth of capacity. They more readily debated topics with passion, took bolder risks with programs and events, and more easily trusted one another's judgments in sensitive areas of ministry.

As part of their organizational reengineering plan, the EMT instituted four lay leadership teams to direct four programmatic ministries in the church: worship, discipleship, evangelism, and service. Those four areas were chosen to coincide with the church's mission statement. After an exhausting process of seeking to identify true leaders within the church, sixteen people agreed to serve on the leadership teams—four per component ministry, so placed because of their deep passion for that ministry component. The EMT then charged each team with developing its own vision to complement and support that of the church at large. After several months of concerted effort, each team enthusiastically produced its vision statement to the EMT for feedback. The vision statements of each team were as follows:

> **Worship Ministry Vision:** To incorporate a genuine worship experience into every public event at the church and to offer other churches and organizations in the area access to our worship capabilities and resources.

> **Discipleship Ministry Vision:** To provide systematic biblical instruction in the context of a meaningful connection with God through teaching, song, and prayer at every church activity.

Evangelism Ministry Vision: To positively influence the lives of non-Christians through worship that provides the presence of God, through significant relationships with worshiping parishioners, and through tailored teaching that demonstrates the relevance of God to non-Christians' lives, leading them into a life-changing relationship with Jesus.

Service Ministry Vision: To reflect God's love and concern through the regular delivery of tangible resources to the needy of the valley as well as personal invitations to worship God with our church family.

Although Pastor Barton was concerned that those statements tended to be a bit wordy, he was visibly moved that each team had so clearly caught the thrust of the church's vision and had so passionately incorporated the worship emphasis into every component ministry. He let the component vision statements stand as they were, with the goal of making them more manageable once each team was immersed in carrying them out. He did not want to discourage his lay-leadership team at this stage by suggesting that their vision was inappropriate. He sensed the heartbeat of each and chose to work with statements whose verbosity was overshadowed by their intensity and intentionality.

Meanwhile, the church's elder board was redefined as a smaller group of godly individuals whose primary responsibility would be to keep the church accountable to its vision and to scriptural principles. The elders were to remain in contact with each leadership team and to serve as spiritual mentors to the church's leaders while also examining the goals, strategies, and tactics of each team to ensure that they reflected biblical integrity. The elders thus transitioned from being a policy-making group—that function was now handled by the EMT and the component ministry teams—to a direct ministry group overseeing prayer, spiritual purity, and congregational care within the church.

As the church settled into this new life, it found that additional lay leaders emerged—some rising from within the congregation and some attracted to the church from the outside. Because the primary component teams had the leaders they needed, the first offer made to new leaders was to serve as apprentices to the existing leaders. After their apprenticeships had been completed, those individuals were then invited to initiate new ministry teams that operated alongside the existing ministry team. For instance, the first new leadership team was a worship team that focused on facilitating worship among the young people in the congregation. The next team added was one that took on responsibility for service ministries to individuals who were immobile, such as prison inmates and shut-ins.

As the leadership capacity of the church grew, so did its attendance and budget, but not its staff. The associate who had been on the payroll when Barton arrived remained for a couple of years, until the transition to team-based ministry was completed, before leaving for another church. The church did hire a new associate whose primary duty was to assist the lay teams that directed the four component ministries. Pastor Barton, meanwhile, reported that he was enjoying ministry more than he had at any prior time in his life—a sentiment echoed by many of his congregants and by nearly all of the church's lay leaders. "It has been an interesting odyssey," he reflected. "I give all the credit to the people in this church who were able to envision what could happen if we took the risk of changing the structure and our entire approach to leadership. We're just an average congregation, I suppose, but we have tremendous team leaders at work here. Their commitment, their gifts, their mutual respect and trust—it has really been a blessing to watch them take the concept and run with it. And it all began with their acceptance of God's vision for us—an enthusiastic, energetic adoption of that simple, eighteen-word statement that has allowed us to add a strategic piece to the ministry puzzle here in the valley."

CHAPTER FOUR

WHY TEAMS ARE SCARCE (AND WHY THEY SHOULDN'T BE)

Few ministry philosophies
I have studied come
as highly recommended
as that of lay-leadership teams.

Churches are among the most predictable subjects on which a researcher can focus. They change slowly—when they change at all—and they are famous for creating and retaining traditions for long periods of time. Without wanting to be pejorative or discouraging, I believe it is safe to predict that most Protestant churches will not incorporate team leadership into their ministry practices in the foreseeable future. In spite of the abundance of compelling reasons to do so (discussed later in this chapter), most will persist in emphasizing solo leadership. Why?

TEN REASONS CHURCHES DON'T USE TEAMS

Our research discovered more than a dozen common reasons why churches either refuse to use leadership teams or have otherwise remained ignorant of the value of team-based leadership. Here's a brief description of ten of the most common reasons.

1. The Desire for Simplicity

Have you ever tried working in a team environment? If you have, then you know firsthand that it's sometimes easier to lead without the encumbrance of other people—even if they generally believe the same things and desire the same ends as you. However, as a team gels over the course of time, the process may become smoother, easier, and even faster than the experience of leading without a team. A variety of research studies show that mature teams typically produce far superior results to what a solo leader is able to achieve. But there is no denying that, at least in the early stages of a team, it may be easier to lead solo than within a team.

Why is this true? In a team, everyone must be on the same page if the job is to be done effectively and efficiently. That requires meetings, discussion, and persuasion—in other words, teamwork often demands more time, energy, and resources to reach the same outcome an individual leader may already embrace.

Our study encountered another common obstacle in this regard: the feeling among many leaders that they will do a better job than anyone else—even if others understand the situation, have useful skills, and want to help. "Look, whenever I get other people involved, yes, there's wider ownership of the process, but the results are just not as good as what I can produce working on my own," explained one pastor. "I can get it done faster, cheaper, smarter, and better. That's not my ego; that's just the truth. People appreciate my ability to get the job done efficiently. That's why they hired me. There are other ways they can use their abilities to serve the church."

Chances are good that this church will never reach its true ministry potential as long as such a person is the primary leader of the ministry, for the church will be limited by that person's capacity to produce results. Not only does such a pastor become a production bottleneck, but he also sends a harmful message to the congregation: Nobody is as good as the pastor, nor can they hope to become as productive. That message has a daunting effect on people's willingness to pull their weight in the church.

2. The Need for Control

Often when a church or program is led by someone who is not truly a leader or by someone who lacks self-confidence or experience, the natural tendency is to dictate what must be done rather than rely upon the wisdom and breadth of experience resident within a group of lay leaders. The result is that creativity is stifled and decisions are limited by the intelligence, sensitivity, and experience of the dictator. Naturally, people are less likely to feel ownership of the choices made for them than if there had been a more inclusive process at work.

It is oppressive to serve within an environment in which one individual controls and dominates. People lose interest, ministry becomes a labor rather than a joy, and results do not reach the heights that might have been achieved within a more inviting process. The controlling leader, however, usually cannot see that reality and dismisses such "complaints" as the narrow-minded, unenlightened views of those who are jealous, power hungry, or immature.

3. The Need for Personal Significance

Whether due to fragile egos or misperception, many leaders eschew the team approach because it reduces the perceived value of the individual. If a team is making decisions and providing leadership, then the individual is no longer the center of attention, thereby minimizing his or her perceived importance to the ministry. Many leaders fight hard to maintain complete authority because they have a deep-seated need to be needed. Whether they feel they are indispensable or have a need to feel so depends upon the person—but the outcome is the same, regardless of the driving motivation.

> *Many leaders fight hard to maintain complete authority because they have a deep-seated need to be needed.*

The bottom line is that the introduction of team-based leadership is a personal threat to such an individual. Rather than focusing upon the good of the ministry, these people look only to what's best for themselves and would rather experience personal status and prestige than do what is right for the ministry.

4. The Quest for Efficiency

How often have you heard someone dismiss the idea of working with others by lightly noting, "I can do it faster by myself"? This is sometimes accurate. After all, a team may require meetings to identify its challenges and tasks, gather information, plan, discuss options, resolve resulting conflict and confusion—in other words, it is likely that more time and energy will be consumed in getting to a point of decision and implementation.

Accepting such an argument, however, assumes that the only significant outcome is to do something—regardless of the quality of the action and its product. Only in exceptional instances is it likely that the results of one person will outweigh the results of a competent team of individuals working together toward a common goal. Achieving the fastest turnaround does not always produce "excellence" in the product.

5. Adherence to Tradition

For the last quarter-century it has become common practice to criticize churches for not trying new methods or ideas. But despite this widespread ridicule of churches' stubborn adherence to outdated traditions and practices, thousands continue to resist reasonable change. It has been said that the seven last words of the church will be "We've never done it that way before."

Using teams as the means of leadership is outside the traditional boundaries of most churches. One pastor clearly expressed his views on this during my conversation with him: "You know, we've been providing godly leadership for our people for seven decades without using this team concept, and we'll probably continue to provide godly leadership for another seven decades without introducing team leadership." The fact that his church had not experienced an increase in attendance or budget in the past decade, that there was an average of less than two conversions per year at his church, or that few people spent any time outside of church services relating to Christ and studying God's Word apparently was irrelevant to him. His church was comfortable with its routine and unconcerned about the results. After all, they were doing what their church had always done. Introducing a team-based leadership approach might be interpreted by some as saying that the church's founders and predecessors had not lived up to their potential.

6. They Don't Know How

Another common argument offered by churches against using teams is that they have never been trained to work as team leaders and therefore cannot make the transition away from solo leadership. Although there are widely accessible team-leadership books, videotapes, conferences, seminars, and other training resources, few pastors and church staff have been exposed to such training. (Interestingly, we discovered that many lay leaders have used such resources as part of their vocational training.) The issue is not really that church leaders cannot get the training they need to create a viable team process, but it is not a priority for them.

Once again, it seems that the excuse masks a deeper reservation; namely, that the individual does not truly embrace the team approach. Given the availability of resources that would facilitate a workable move toward team leadership, not knowing how to make the change is a weak excuse but one that we found many pastors offer as a daunting obstacle.

7. Nobody Models It

Some church leaders noted that they do not work within leadership teams because they have not seen it modeled for them in other churches. This concern generally means either that team leadership is not sufficiently widespread to qualify, in their eyes, as a practice worth replicating, or that there exists no credible example of team leadership from which they could learn. Either way, this excuse highlights one of the unfortunate diseases that characterize many churches: ministry by mimicry.

Our studies over the past ten years have shown that when an organization lacks strong leadership, the tendency is to find a competing or similar organization that is successful and copy whatever that group seems to be doing. This strategy rarely works for the imitator, because it does not understand the underlying structure and the different context within which the successful entity operates. Further, the imitator typically tries to implement a facsimile of the original model in a very compressed period of time, effectively precluding the church from truly grasping the foundational ministry philosophy that allowed the process to work in the church where it originated.

The idea that team leadership has not been witnessed in other ministries raises two concerns. First, most church leaders do not actually get to scrutinize the operations and ministry activity of other churches. The typical pastor or staff person attends an average of one or two seminars or conferences per year. Often, those are events sponsored by very large churches of national reputation (for example, Willow Creek Community Church, Saddleback Community Church, First Assembly of Phoenix), which means that their exposure to ministry is limited to a few wonderful but atypical churches. Second, the absence of exposure to team leadership reminds us that there are not enough churches engaging in this practice to make it a visible and noticeable element in almost any church whose ministry is being observed or studied.

8. *Absence of Vision*

Leadership teams serve within the boundaries of the macro-level vision cast by the primary leaders of the organization. One of the barriers to using teams, then, is the absence of vision within a church. A survey we conducted several years ago showed that very few pastors (less than one in ten) were able to articulate God's vision for their church. The consequence is that their churches are not really going anywhere special, unique, or significant; they are simply ministry outposts doing good works without an understanding of their unique and necessary role within the kingdom.

If a church without a clear vision tried to fashion a team-based leadership process, toward what goal would those teams lead the church? Without a clear vision, they have no destination. The only real objective would be to help the church survive, which is the antithesis of godly leadership. God's leaders exist to facilitate spiritual transformation and maturity; encouraging believers and a congregation to accept a spiritual holding pattern is unscriptural and requires no leadership.

9. The Pastor's Traditional, Central Role

In a team environment, the leadership role of the pastor shifts from that of leading the entire congregation to being a leader of leaders. This is exactly the role Jesus exemplified: Rather than shepherd the thousands, He shepherded the twelve who then led the throngs who were attracted to the Lord. This team-leadership model reduces the stress on the pastor from having to be all things to all people and essentially becoming nothing to everyone. The pastor may instead pour whatever he or she has to offer into a relative handful of fellow leaders, who in turn provide the breadth and depth of leadership that the church requires.

Despite its obvious advantages, for thousands of pastors such a transition is improbable. They were raised to believe that the pastor leads everyone and must have direct, unfettered oversight of the masses. The problem is that if a leader clings to that perspective, he or she will never have the chance to lead masses in the first place, because people who are serious about spiritual growth simply will not put up with what amounts to superficial leadership.

Perhaps we can adapt an old axiom and posit that it takes a mature person to embrace team leadership, because it demands giving up the spotlight, the authority, and the view of the pastor as the center of all church activity.

10. Church Culture

As we will discuss later in this book, making the move to teams will fail unless the transition happens within the context of a church culture that demands and esteems teamwork. You cannot simply accept the idea of team leadership and try to implement it within an operational structure that is not designed to facilitate teams or within a culture that does not resonate with teamwork.

Every organization, including your church, has an operating culture. That culture is comprised of all of the symbols, traditions, assumptions, customs, ideals, values, language, and systems that interpret and deliver your ministry reality. Culture is what gives context and meaning to your experience. That culture is continually evolving, but once its foundation has been laid, it takes extraordinary effort and intentionality to modify it.

Most churches would rather live within the confines of an unhealthy culture than go through the painstaking transformation a cultural shift requires. If your church has always used solo leadership, becoming a team-led church would demand a complete rethinking of many core values and practices such as defining the role of the pastor, delegating responsibility and authority, establishing accountability, developing true community, determining priorities and goals, and creating a viable organizational structure.

WELL WORTH THE EFFORT

Do any of those ten justifications for avoiding team leadership reign within your church? If so, please think and pray about the implications of refusing to use a process that has so often proven to be more effective than its alternatives.

Indisputably, shifting from solo leadership to team leadership is a major transition and will bring with it all of the challenges common to making any significant change in behavior and philosophy. But I want to encourage you by affirming that the pastors and church staff we talked with who have blazed the trail before you *unanimously* indicated that the hard work was well worth the effort.

Few ministry philosophies I have studied come as highly recommended as that of lay-leadership teams. "I can tell you all the benefits we have experienced from switching to teams," explained the senior pastor of one of the churches we studied. "At the time we changed over [from solo leadership] I had some doubts about it being a smart thing to do. It didn't happen overnight, and the transition wasn't without its moments of frustration and disappointment. But to be honest, I can't remember a single one of those doubts today. That probably speaks volumes to the fact that the advantages have been so overwhelming that I can't even recall what my concerns were. This transition has been a total win-win situation for us."

TEN REASONS CHURCHES SHOULD USE TEAM LEADERSHIP

At the start of this chapter I mentioned that I would identify some compelling reasons to incorporate a team-leadership approach. Hopefully, you can already sense that the dominant objections and obstacles to team leadership are indefensible excuses. To strengthen the argument in favor of team leadership—and perhaps your resolve to move toward a team-based ministry—let me present ten benefits of using team leadership in your ministry.

1. Biblical Endorsement

Our ministry principles and methods should be consistent with the Bible. In studying the lives of God's chosen leaders portrayed in Scripture, we find a variety of models. Jesus devoted His years of public ministry to developing a team of leaders who then led the early church after His death and resurrection. Paul was a devoted team practitioner, traveling with various teams. Moses led in tandem with Joshua and Aaron by his side. David and Nehemiah may be included among the other leaders who worked with teams.

The Bible does not give a direct admonition to provide team-based leadership, but it does teach the value of community, unity, diversity, mutual trust, and the interrelationship of spiritual gifts—all aspects that lead to a team-based approach. Looking at the issue from a different angle, the Word clearly teaches that we are not to be independent of God nor overly self-confident nor strive to accomplish things in our own strength and power. Again, such a perspective moves us closer to embracing a team-oriented strategy for growing the church, because it teaches us to look outward, not inward.

2. No More Superheroes

The oft-heard complaint that "There just aren't enough lay leaders to make the church's ministry happen" is not an accurate representation of the situation. What we lack are the dynamic, high-energy, driven, charismatic, compelling leaders who have become icons of our culture—individuals such as Jack Welch, Ronald Reagan, Lee Iacocca, Steve Jobs, and Peter Ueberroth. In the church world we elevate extraordinary leaders such as Bill Hybels, Rick Warren, Kirbyjon Caldwell, Paul Cho, Jack Hayford, and Ted Haggard to that same level of leadership "superstardom." But most people do not have the mix of gifts, talent, experience, and opportunity that has enabled these individuals to gain notoriety.

> *God has provided us with all the leaders we need*
> *to accomplish the aims of the church.*

The fact that few people possess such incredible leadership capacity is an important realization, for it means that most churches are resigned to one of two outcomes: consistent failure due to the lack of available high-impact leaders or reliance upon a different leadership paradigm. Given our understanding that God takes pleasure in His people succeeding, that He never sets up His followers for failure, and that the church is God's instrument for ministry throughout the world, we can confidently assert that He has provided us with all the leaders we need to accomplish the aims of the church. Therefore, we ought to recognize that the prevailing idea about leadership—namely, that people are to be led only by powerhouse individual leaders—is simply wrong.

Once we embrace the idea that leadership can be capably (and often more capably) provided by teams, then we can shed our inferiority complexes and stop looking for superheroes.

Instead, we must help every believer identify his or her gifts and abilities and release those with the gift of leadership to serve people through that God-given capacity. As management pioneer Peter Drucker sagely observed, "The purpose of a team is to make the strengths of each person effective and his or her weaknesses irrelevant."[1]

3. True Community

A hallmark of an authentic Christian church is that its people are not merely acquaintances who share a sanctuary once a week, but that they are a community of people who believe the same things, follow the same Lord, and love one another. Since the congregation often takes its cues from the church's leaders, it is important that the leaders be united, trust and support one another, and serve in harmony. There is no better way to foster such leadership than in a team environment.

One of the beautiful outcomes of lay leadership within teams is that the congregation quickly understands that ministry is done by the laity and that the church exemplifies cooperation in the performance of its duties. That is a key message for the congregation to absorb: We are one in vision, in relationship, and in ministry as modeled by our church leaders.

4. Less Stress

If we can reduce the burden of leadership shouldered by church leaders, one outcome would be a reduction in the stress levels they feel. While Scripture alludes to the hardships of ministry, it does not suggest that we must add to the pressures of living a holy and servant-based life by placing incredible—sometimes unreasonable—expectations upon mere mortals. One viable means of reducing stress levels is by working in teams.

Leadership, by its very nature, will produce stress. Whenever you seek to motivate people to change the way they think or live, stress will emerge. Whenever you make decisions that affect people's lives, you will experience the stress of responsibility. Whenever you battle the forces of evil for the glory of God, stress will be a by-product of the battle. Stress is an unavoidable hazard that leaders cope with from the time they begin leading until they retire from such service. In fact, one of the characteristics of effective leaders is that they can handle the stress and pressure they encounter as they fulfill their leadership obligations.

Team-oriented leadership does not eliminate stress, but it does reduce it by sparing the individual from having to be the expert in everything. The work load is shared, the decision making is carried out in cooperation with other skilled and insightful partners, and the gifts required to do an excellent job are resident within the team. The anxiety that comes from recognizing that you are in over your head may not be completely eliminated; after all, God's desire is that we rely upon Him for our strength and direction. If it became too easy, we'd become independent and arrogant. Team leaders can serve with greater assurance and serenity because of the strength of the team.

5. Greater Synergy

"One of the lessons I finally absorbed is that a team always out-performs an individual, no matter how gifted that individual may be," declared one pastor we interviewed. "I used to pride myself on my ability to get things done and to get people excited about what I'd done, but eventually I burned out and realized that if I had simply opened my eyes, recognized the warehouse of talent the Lord brought here, and allowed other people to use their abilities, we'd all be better off. Our teams don't just increase the impact of the leaders, they multiply them several times over."

A true team generates results far greater than the sum of the parts could have achieved. One of the ways you can tell if a team is firing on all cylinders is by evaluating its output. If it substantially exceeds what would have occurred had the team members been leading on a solo basis, then the team is functional. If the team is merely producing results equal to what they would have produced if each individual were working independently, then the team is not at its optimal level. (There are various reasons for that shortfall—inappropriate matching of aptitudes, an inferior captain, an ambiguous process—all of which we will discuss later.)

> *"Our teams don't just increase the impact of the leaders, they multiply them several times over."*

One of the great joys of team leadership is participating in a synergistic process. "It's like a bonus," exclaimed one of the lay leaders to whom we spoke. "After a while, you just enjoy working with these other people so much that you can't imagine leading any other way, but then when you see the results shoot off the chart, well, you start to realize that the combined efforts of properly matched leaders can produce unimaginable results."

6. More Innovation

Leaders solve problems. Great leaders solve problems creatively, enabling them to overcome a broader range of problems and to devise lasting solutions to vexing challenges. Imagine what happens when you team a group of creative problem solvers who embrace the same vision. The result is a plethora of new ideas, a higher level of innovative thinking, and a heightened willingness to take reasonable risks that may launch the ministry to another level of impact.

As our culture becomes more complicated and people's attention and energy is diverted from the things of God, we will need more creative responses to engage people in spiritual development and ministry. A great idea is a great idea, whether it comes from one person or from a team. But the evidence indicates that the push-pull dynamic that occurs among a group of individuals with a shared commitment is likely to outdistance anything that the lone-ranger leader conceives.

7. Greater Joy

People love to succeed. Leadership, being the challenging calling that it is, provides its practitioners with an emotional and spiritual high when they experience victories en route to their ultimate destination.

Leading as a team, though, produces a superior sense of joy. Why? Just as a loving parent experiences more profound joy over a family achievement than a personal one, so a team leader feels greater joy when the team facilitates a positive outcome. In other words, participation in a team process often becomes a reward in itself through the distinctive experiences that emerge from the group process and relationships.

Not surprisingly, we also found that the results derived through team efforts may exceed those that would have been achieved through individual effort, further increasing the satisfaction through teamwork.

8. *The Priesthood of Believers*

Team-based leadership is surely an extension of the Ephesians 4 exhortation to equip the saints for ministry, in the same way that Peter and John discussed the importance of believers forming a priesthood of believers who serve together.[2]

God has entrusted a wealth of resources to His people—spiritual gifts, money, time, relationships, material possessions, opportunities, ideas, information—for the purpose of knowing, loving, and serving Him. In fact, team-oriented ministry is one of the means of deploying the gifts that people possess for maximum ministry potential. But just as Paul wrote that no one person has all of the spiritual gifts given by God, neither does any one individual have all the attributes necessary to lead with perfection. It is through mutual reliance that leaders achieve their highest potential.

9. Facilitates Numerical Growth

Churches that exhibit great leadership grow because the people attending those churches understand the vision of the church, are motivated to participate in the fulfillment of that vision, are encouraged to use their unique gifts and abilities to contribute to the church's ministry, are teamed with others whose gifts and skills complement their own, and are encouraged to develop the resources required to have the desired impact. People are attracted to strong visionary leadership. Churches that provide such direction and support are magnetic, invariably growing both numerically as well as spiritually.

> *The dynamic teaching or charismatic personality of a pastor can take a church only so far.*

Unfortunately, many large churches lose their spiritual edge because their leaders fail to deputize lay leaders to push the church to its potential. The dynamic teaching or charismatic personality of a pastor can take a church only so far. Such individuals may attract large numbers of people, but unless they provide true leadership, which facilitates spiritual transformation, the church will simply become a religious event center with increasingly demanding observers. When congregants who have been called by God to lead are brought together in teams and given the responsibility and authority to lead, the ministry becomes decentralized and is thus capable of increased growth—numerical and spiritual.

10. Relieves the Senior Pastor

Most churches remain wholly dependent upon the abilities and energy of the senior pastor. When teams take over the leadership load, the pastor is freed to deliver what he or she has uniquely been called and gifted to bring to the church. In team-led churches we discovered that pastors enjoy their vocation more, stay at their churches longer, and are less prone to burnout. Their churches are spiritually healthier too.

TEAMS MAKE SENSE

Can you understand why every church we interviewed that has gone the team-leadership route raves about the impact? Team leadership makes sense, but it also has a proven track record in practice. Developing a workable team process is neither quick nor easy, but with the right level of commitment and resources, the transition is likely to be well worth the effort.

But what does it take to pull this off successfully? Our study showed that developing great team leadership is a matter of how you work with your people, the process you implement and sustain, and the product you seek. In the next chapter we'll explore the experience of churches that have done this successfully.

CHAPTER FIVE

THE PEOPLE
FACTOR IN TEAM
DEVELOPMENT

*Look for people who have
the calling, the character, and
the competencies to lead effectively.*

Your church might have the best facilities in town, the greatest opportunities for impact, and the most efficient systems in place, but without the right people, none of those conditions make much difference.

"It took me years to realize that although I understood the process of leadership development, I didn't have much understanding of who the right people were to invite into leadership," confessed one veteran Presbyterian pastor in Michigan. "Once I focused on getting the right people involved, everything started to click."

As you identify people for involvement in leadership teams at your church, you will save yourself and your church much stress and turmoil if you know what you're looking for from the start. You are seeking *leaders,* which means individuals who have been called by God to lead, who have godly character, and who possess the competencies to help people fulfill God's vision for the group. In addition, you are seeking to combine people of compatible leadership aptitudes and who have the ability to work effectively in a team setting. Let's examine each of these areas more closely.

CALLED BY GOD

Our highest calling, of course, is to be disciples, doing whatever it takes to live according to His will for His followers. But every Christian is also called by God to serve Him in a unique fashion, exploiting the gifts, talents, abilities, experiences, passions, and opportunities He has provided. When we take advantage of opportunities to serve Him within our area of calling we provide a unique, desirable, and valued addition to His kingdom. We experience a heightened degree of satisfaction in ministry, and the recipients of such ministry also derive true benefit from the experience.

But while God calls every Christian to a role of service (Romans 12:4-8), not everyone is called to be a leader (1 Corinthians 12:12-27). In fact, most people we read about in the Bible were not leaders, but they served important roles within the development of God's kingdom. He calls each believer to fill a special role in His work, and corporately we fill a variety of roles within His kingdom. Each of those roles must be adequately fulfilled for His church to realize its fullness.

The tension, of course, is that some people aspire to leadership even though God has neither called nor gifted them for such a position within His service. Churches often ignore the obvious mismatch between godly calling and human desire, which results in an awkward and sometimes harmful disparity of role and servant. Clearly and accurately knowing the nature of your calling is crucial, for unshakable certainty will motivate you to persist in the face of resistance and challenges. Such conviction is especially important for those who believe they are called to lead. That particular calling is given to a select group of believers for the purpose of guiding God's people toward the fulfillment of the distinct vision He has given to them collectively as well as the unique vision He provides to each believer individually. The call to lead is not superior to other roles to which people may be called, but the breadth of responsibility assigned to leaders demands that they be quite certain that God intends for them to serve in such a manner.

A calling is typically affirmed through several conditions. *First, after extensive and intensive prayer, Bible study, and self-assessment, the individual senses God's calling to lead.* When God calls a person to a task, it is imperative that he or she has conviction about it—for without a deep passion for that work, the chances of having a significant impact are limited. Passion for the specific ministry calling enables a person to transcend the inevitable obstacles and difficulties related to accomplishing God's tasks.

Second, the calling should be affirmed by those who know the individual well. If they do not endorse the calling as reasonable, further exploration is warranted. However, if the people who know the individual most intimately acknowledge the likelihood of his or her call to leadership, such support represents a strong endorsement. Throughout Scripture the individuals whom God called to be leaders were accepted by the people they were to lead, thereby strengthening the claim of their calling.

Third, a called individual will possess the requisite spiritual gifts and leadership skills. Often those gifts and skills need to be refined, but the presence of those resources in the individual is additional evidence of God's plan for the person. There is some contention among Christians as to which spiritual gifts a person should have in order to be an effective leader. Our research suggests that the gifts most likely to characterize a called leader are those within the group of "directive gifts" that enable a believer to direct the activities of individuals and groups within the body of Christ. The three directive gifts are *leadership, apostleship,* and *pastoring.* Individuals who have been granted these gifts generally provide comprehensive, vision-based direction that empowers and enhances the lives of others.

> *Recognizing people's call to leadership is the starting point in identifying who should be involved in leadership teams.*

Fourth, the person's life experience reflects a tendency to serve as a leader, no matter what the circumstances might be. I have noticed over the years that leaders cannot help but lead. Even when they are not in leadership positions, they cannot restrain their natural abilities to motivate, mobilize, direct, and resource people to pursue a compelling vision. When such leadership is not provided by others, it grates on them until they step forward to assume some level of leadership.

Recognizing people's call to leadership is the starting point in identifying who should be involved in leadership teams. If the call is not clear, work with these individuals to get a better sense of who God made them to be. Help them dig deeper in self-discovery to learn more about God's design for their lives. But do not give them leadership assignments before you are confident that leadership is the role that God intends them to fill. Trying to convert nonleaders into leaders is a painful experience for the wannabe leader as well as for those who will suffer through their misadventure.

GODLY IN CHARACTER

Human character reflects who we really are. The Bible is pretty clear that all of us are sinners who are crippled by the effects of sin. In spite of that handicap, God uses His followers for His ends and chooses some to be leaders. A key to fulfilling that calling is to have a heart for becoming more like Christ. All believers are expected to possess such character, but it may become a more sensitive issue for Christian leaders because they become role models to the world as well as to their churches by virtue of their visibility and influence.

A worldly leader ascends the ladder of authority because of what he or she accomplishes. A godly leader is granted the privilege of leading God's people because he or she has a heart to know, love, and serve God by leading His people to fulfill His vision. As a result of that burning desire to serve in this way, and to honor God at all times by modeling righteousness and holy living, people are motivated to follow such a leader. Leadership becomes effective on the basis of character rather than salesmanship or style. In fact, leaders have their greatest influence on the basis of two special elements: the vision they convey and the character they possess. Without a compelling cause to support, a leader will generate little interest. Without attractive, godly character, a leader cannot generate confidence among the people.

Every great leader of God exhibits the brand of character attributed to David, "a man after my [God's] own heart" (Acts 13:22). The Bible clearly outlines the character traits that enable a person to be a Christian leader. While none of us is a perfect reflection of all those traits, we are to be generally consistent with, and constantly moving toward, a more godly and righteous character. Harboring glaring character deficiencies or a stubborn refusal to submit to the Holy Spirit and the shaping influence of godly mentors disqualifies an individual from church leadership—no matter how skilled or talented that individual might be in leadership competencies. The kingdom of God is never so desperate for leaders that biblical standards should be relaxed to accommodate a person of skills and high potential. God always cares more about who we are than about what we accomplish.

Perhaps the best recitation of the character qualities of Christian leaders is located in 1 Timothy 3, which I encourage every pastor to keep before him while selecting potential candidates for his leadership team. As you search for individuals who will provide

THE PEOPLE FACTOR IN TEAM DEVELOPMENT

excellent leadership within your church, examine the character of each to see how it measures up against the attributes Paul listed. You will never find a perfect match, but you will discover that God has brought your church many individuals who thirst for the holy lifestyle that Paul describes. If God is the potter, rest assured that there is good clay waiting to be molded into effective leaders for Him.

POSSESSES LEADERSHIP COMPETENCIES

Competencies are the accumulation of skills, knowledge, experiences, and abilities that allow a leader to lead well. In a ministry context, competencies are the actions taken by leaders to intentionally and strategically facilitate positive life transformations toward Christlikeness. Competencies are the outgrowth of a Christian leader's determining to serve God through leadership (calling), being in tune with God and thus knowing where to lead His people (vision), attracting followers through a demonstration of God's work in his or her life (character), and striving to provide people with the direction and tools they need to facilitate God-honoring change and growth.

For a leader to be effective, he or she must possess and utilize an array of competencies. Those skills combine to become the tools of the leader, and the more tools the leader has, the greater the capacity to produce significant results. Unlike calling, competencies can be taught. Unlike character, the absence of particular competencies does not disqualify a God-ordained leader from serving. You will likely find that most leaders within your church have raw talent that needs to be recognized and refined. If the individual has been called by God to lead and reflects and longs for Christlike character, investing in his or her development as a leader is worthwhile.

> *Most leaders within your church have raw talent*
> *that needs to be recognized and refined.*

Since competencies are the actual efforts and abilities leaders deploy to motivate, mobilize, resource, and direct people toward fulfilling the vision God has provided for a group of believers, what are those competencies? There are several dozen that could be identified, but here is a brief description of fifteen leadership competencies that seem to be most crucial to the toolbox of effective ministry leaders.

1. Identifying, Articulating, and Casting God's Vision

The basic currency of leaders is vision. It is the light at the end of the tunnel to which every leader directs people, and it is the outcome that creates enthusiasm and hope in the minds and hearts of leaders and followers alike. Every leader must learn to identify God's unique vision for the ministry to which he or she has been called. Every leader must be able to persuasively share that vision with others and to motivate them to join the effort to make the vision a reality. Every leader must exploit every opportunity to communicate that vision far and wide and enlist people in the movement to bring God's ultimate plan to fruition. Remember: Without vision at the center of one's leadership, there is nothing to lead people to—and, consequently, the individual is not truly a leader.

2. Coaching and Developing Other Leaders

While there is a difference between teachers and leaders, we have observed that once leaders have absorbed enough skill and perspective to pass along, they are always mentoring other leaders. The notion of the master-apprentice relationship is usually evident in the lives of leaders: If they are not serving as an apprentice to a more skilled leader, then they are serving as a master leader tutoring those who wish to become more mature in their own competencies. Great leaders recognize that their position and ability are gifts from God to be shared with others for the common good. Effective leaders seek ways to delegate both responsibility and authority to those capable of handling those elements.

3. Developing and Communicating Strategies

Communicating vision without also providing tangible ways to convert the vision into reality breeds frustration. Effective leaders must be able to break the vision into component pieces and develop strategies for implementing the vision. Those component pieces become discussion elements and assignments to be embraced by the people who serve the church.

4. Motivating People to Get Involved

A leader without followers is not really a leader. For the vision to become reality, people must become enthusiastic about the vision and the opportunity to fulfill God's plan. Leaders motivate people through God's vision and personal character and by providing people with realistic and doable tasks to bring the vision to pass. This implies the building of relationships, an effective communications process and a means of reinforcing people's participation in the cause.

5. Efficiently Mobilizing Ministry Participants

The energy and abilities of those who will cooperate in the pursuit of the vision must be efficiently orchestrated to facilitate the grand outcomes that leaders propose. Understanding people's gifts and abilities, recognizing their experience, and blending people into significant work teams is a key role of leaders. This entails the strategic allocation of resources, responsibility, and power. But even more important, a great leader is one who is able to empower people to grow and serve at their fullest capacity. Rallying people around a compelling vision and turning them loose, with direction, to pursue that vision is a critical dimension of leading people.

6. Resolving Conflict

Every team experiences conflict. Effective teams are prepared to handle the conflict and address the issues without allowing the related tensions to undermine the team or its efforts. Conflict resolution demands mutual trust, commitment to the team's vision that transcends the importance of personal goals, a viable process for communication, and a heartfelt desire to maintain strong bonds within the group. The team must also be committed to acknowledging the existence of unhealthy tension and facing the situation before it festers.

7. Identifying, Accumulating, and Utilizing Resources Appropriately

No matter how enthusiastic the team may be, little can be accomplished without adequate resources. There are many types of resources: financial, human, spiritual, material. Leaders must be able to recruit or acquire the resources needed to get the job done. In addition, leaders must be good stewards of the resources the Lord entrusts to them. The wise allocation and use of resources and a genuine spirit of gratitude for their availability are vital to effective leadership.

> *Leaders must be able to read the signs*
> *of discouragement, weariness, and dissipating trust.*

8. Reinforcing Commitment and Success

God's vision is never easy to achieve. People will experience substantial challenges and even temporary defeats along the path to success, and such barriers may discourage them. Because we live in a busy society and most Christians are trying to fit their faith into an already-overwhelming schedule, individuals often become frustrated or fatigued. Leaders must be able to read the signs of discouragement, weariness, and dissipating trust to keep people excited about the special role they play in the process. Similarly, when victories are achieved, it is important for leaders to supply appropriate reinforcement and celebration.

9. Objectively Evaluating the Ministry

Progress demands an accurate sense of where you stand. Leaders must constantly know the pulse of the people and have a clear comprehension of what strategies are and are not working as well as how much farther the endeavor must go to achieve its ends. Leaders have a responsibility to protect people from failure whenever possible. But because they also have a responsibility to ensure that the ministry is operating at a level of excellence, some means of consistent evaluation of both quality and productivity is a key tool for effective leadership.

10. Intentionally Shaping the Corporate Culture

As noted in the previous chapter, every ministry develops an internal culture that greatly impacts its ability to generate meaningful outcomes. Leaders must purposefully shape the culture of the ministry, integrating appropriate values, language, customs, systems, priorities, goals, and behavioral standards. The culture facilitates desired outcomes as well as provides parameters within which the ministry's adherents will live.

11. Modeling Christian Character and Commitment

Because people tend to imitate the attitudes and actions of others they respect, leaders are usually among those from whom the masses take their cues. Thus it is imperative that a leader's commitment to Christ, to His vision for the ministry, and to growing in Christlike character shine brightly. A true leader is not one who says, "Do as I say, not as I do," but one who needs to say little because his or her actions speak for themselves. To lead in ministry, an individual should possess obvious spiritual maturity and genuine dedication to growing deeper in Christian faith. Great Christian leaders are authentically loving and caring people and are not afraid to be "real" and vulnerable. Their integrity and humility must run deep.

12. Attracting and Maintaining an Effective Team

Leaders love to be with other leaders. They are always on the lookout for others who possess the same passion, gifting, and calling that they have. Providing fellow leaders with opportunities to contribute to the cause is a personal joy and a corporate benefit. Once those individuals become part of the leadership family, maintaining healthy work and personal relationships is an important priority.

13. Leading by Serving

Perhaps the most profound leadership lesson Jesus gave to His apprentices was that a leader is not the first among people but the servant of all people. In a culture that fosters independence and personal achievement, leadership that focuses on addressing the needs of others is a foreign concept. Christian leaders must emulate the example of Jesus and pour themselves into building up and edifying the body of believers so that they, too, might devote themselves to selflessly serving others—that is, expressing the distinctives of a genuine, Christian love.

14. Solving Problems and Meeting Challenges

People turn to their leaders for direction, resources, strength, and encouragement in the face of problems. A leader must have the capacity to study a situation, interpret the findings intelligently, conceive a strategic course of action, marshal the resources to implement the response, and monitor progress and make midcourse adjustments as necessary. In the same way, when nonproblematic challenges arise, a leader must know which to pursue and which to ignore.

15. Clarifying and Promoting Core Values

Defining what is worthy, important, and appropriate—that is, *values*—is a central function of an effective leader. Those values influence our culture, our character, our hopes for the future, and our present-day behavior and morals. Internal consistency is a hallmark of effective leaders, but such consistency is not attainable unless a clear delineation of values is provided and upheld.

Undoubtedly you can think of other important competencies leaders must possess to help their churches succeed. These fifteen attributes are not meant to be an exhaustive list but to reflect what we have observed to be the most significant competencies in the lives of effective leaders. As you evaluate the people who might serve in leadership capacities in your church, do they possess these competencies? If not, are they willing to develop them? Do they have the ability to grow in these areas?

Let's be honest: Every leader does not shine with equal brightness in each of these dimensions. As we examine the four leadership aptitudes in the next chapter, we will discover that every leader excels in some areas and performs only adequately in others. Being able to recognize those relative strengths and weaknesses will become a critical element in developing effective teams.

CHAPTER SIX # CHAPTER SIX

THE FOUR LEADERSHIP APTITUDES

---

*Don't look for team leaders
of similar aptitudes; look for those
with complementary aptitudes.*

Just as schoolteachers specialize in certain subjects, so do leaders have certain dimensions of leadership in which they are more proficient. The act of leading people and organizations covers a lot of ground. It is not reasonable to expect one individual to have all of the abilities, information, skills, gifts, and experiences that would enable him or her to lead effectively. It is that very expectation, of course, that gets many churches into trouble as they search for a "superhero" leader.

Every leader has what we have labeled a "dominant leadership aptitude," which refers to a specialization or emphasis within the leadership endeavor. A leadership aptitude is more than a style of leading; it incorporates a specific skill set, personality type, and strategic perspective that moves the leader to emphasize or excel in one particular aspect of leadership more than the other aspects that comprise aggregate leadership.

Understanding leadership aptitudes and incorporating that knowledge into the development of the individual leader and into the blending and training of each team is crucial to success. Often, we found that churches arrive at this understanding through a painful combination of intuition and trial and error. Our study of leadership dynamics may help you shorten the process without losing any of the outcomes.

There are four leadership aptitudes. Some leaders are best in the *directing* aspect of leadership. Others are best at the *strategic development* required for impact. Many leaders thrive on the *interpersonal* dimension of leadership and specialize in building networks and teams. Still others are at their best when they create *systems* that facilitate effective leadership and ministry. Because each of these approaches to leadership requires a different way of viewing reality, a different type of relationship with people, and a distinct set of skills within the leadership domain, it is not possible for any one individual to be the "complete" leader. In fact, if you possessed all four of these aptitudes, the best description of you might be "clinically schizophrenic." You would always be at war with yourself as you strive to see the world from disparate points of view. You would be frustrated in developing relationships that serve leadership productivity and also overwhelmed by the breadth of output that must be delivered to move the ministry toward the fulfillment of its vision.

The upshot of this realization is that the ideal team is comprised of four leaders, each representing a different aptitude. In fact, we have seen time after time that the absence of any one of the four aptitudes renders the ministry vulnerable and unstable. A team that blends these four aptitudes has the potential to accomplish great things for the kingdom with excellence, efficacy, and efficiency.

> *The ideal team is comprised of four leaders,*
> *each representing a different aptitude.*

But what do these people look like? How do you know who represents each of these qualities? As you read the following profiles of the four types of leaders—their primary contribution to the team effort, their strengths, their weaknesses—see if you recognize any individuals who minister and worship alongside you every week.

1. The Directing Leader

Ronald Reagan was the quintessential *directing leader*. These individuals excel at conveying a compelling vision but do not invest their energy in the details of the process. They motivate people to get involved in or feel encouraged by the appealing future they describe and the significant role the people can play in bringing that future to pass. These leaders rally people around the cause and get other leaders to understand and own the direction that they will jointly pursue to fulfill the vision.

Directing leaders are catalysts. They excite people's imaginations and enable them to believe in themselves. That motivational capacity attracts people to the cause. Directing leaders are effective public speakers and good listeners. They make people feel as if they matter.

Directing leaders are good decision makers. They like to have the facts at their disposal, but as often as not their decisions are based on their "gut"—their instincts are good and they have a life-long track record of success based upon their reliance on intuition. They do not shrink from the tough calls; it is during times of high stress or instability and uncertainty that the wisdom and courage of directing leaders becomes most evident. These leaders are sensitive to the values and beliefs that drive their worldview, and they shudder at the notion of compromising their core values.

Like everyone, directing leaders have weaknesses. Among those are their disinterest in the minutiae of the process. They exhibit little patience for discussions about details and are not likely to labor over plans that address contingencies—although they often insist that those details be thought through and strategically addressed. When a directing leader is not accompanied by a more detail-oriented colleague, chaos results. Often you will find that directing leaders are great with large groups of people but not especially warm with individuals. They also tend to be restless, have short attention spans, favor action over reflection, and may ignore financial limitations and realities. Their interest is in making good things happen—now!—and they show little appetite for debating the ins and outs of the route that will get them where they need to go.

2. *The Strategic Leader*

Generally speaking, *strategic leaders* are individuals who are content to remain in the background and evaluate the options that lie before the organization, eventually developing detailed plans of action that address the key needs and opportunities. Strategic leaders are more comfortable at creating the practical means of converting vision into action than they are at pumping up the people with the big picture.

Strategic leaders are analysts of reality: They observe people and situations and collect empirical information, then they run it through their mental grid to arrive at conclusions about the real conditions and opportunities of the world. They remain sufficiently detached to arrive at objective conclusions. Many strategic leaders view emotions and sensitivity as detrimental to the cause. Their allegiance is to truth and efficiency in making the vision reality.

Strategic leaders tend to be very thorough in their investigations and do not hesitate to ask the hard questions. They don't mind creating controversy, because their primary quest is to understand reality in order to develop a workable plan. Once they have amassed the facts and carefully analyzed them, strategic leaders are prone to develop creative, albeit sometimes complex solutions.

These individuals are more loyal to the vision than they are to people. They also take great pride in being well versed in their area of focus. It is rare to find a strategic leader at a loss to explain something; however, if strategic leaders do not know the answer, such a deficiency fuels their zest for further discovery. Strategic leaders almost always overprepare for meetings. Should you ask them a question, you are likely to get more detail than you care to hear—unless, of course, you are a strategic leader too.

Typically, strategic leaders are seen as useful, but generally they are not the most popular leaders. Because they focus on facts, figures, plans, and possibilities, they are sometimes portrayed as being insensitive or unemotional, even robotic. The truth is that they do have feelings and do care for people, but they know that they cannot trust feelings to arrive at useful conclusions. They are usually happier working with ideas than with people.

A common complaint about strategic leaders is that they take so long to arrive at decisions. This is frequently because they hate to make a decision without having complete information on which to base their judgment. These are people who believe they can eliminate all risks in decision making if they can just analyze enough data. Unfortunately, nobody ever gets that much data. This tendency also points to a leaning toward perfectionism that sometimes undermines the efforts of the strategic leader.

3. The Team-Building Leader

While directing leaders love the energy involved in chasing the dream and strategic leaders love the intellectual challenge of understanding and planning, *team-building leaders* love people. Their primary strength is their ability to interact with a wide variety of people and leave everyone feeling that they have been heard, understood, and loved.

Of the four types of leaders, team-building leaders are best at mobilizing people around the vision through relational context.

They love to organize people around a common cause. They work their relational network to bring together individuals who share passion for the outcomes and who are likely to enjoy working together. In the process of building these new coalitions, team builders leave everyone feeling good about themselves, their team, and their potential to produce something significant. The team-building leader is the life of the party—or, in the case of a ministry activity, the popular, trusted friend of all whose charisma and personality encourage those in the trenches to give it their best shot.

Team-building leaders love people but hate paperwork. The stories are legion of such leaders who have made a shambles of well-constructed ministry strategies by simply ignoring anything that was put on paper—action plans, operational budgets, ministry assignments, or agendas. In fact, team-building leaders have a tendency to waffle on details. You will also find that their strength—relationships—is also their weakness, because they often get burned by investing too much trust and confidence in people who do not (or sometimes cannot) come through as promised.

4. The Operational Leader

Operational leaders provide a degree of stability, predictability, and consistency to the activity of the ministry. They focus upon the operations of the ministry, but they do so as leaders, not as managers. That's a major distinction. *Managers* lean toward maintaining and improving what exists; *leaders* emphasize creating new opportunities and solutions that result in breakthroughs. Operational leaders, then, conceive and introduce new routines designed to facilitate the accomplishment of the vision.

Operational leaders may be low-key and virtually invisible, but their contribution is indispensable. In the wake of the chaos and roadblocks generated by the other three types of leaders, a structural architect is needed to enable ministry to flow efficiently. Thus operational leaders devise systems that make things run smoothly. They may also serve as the hub through which all activity is coordinated to ensure that there are no loose ends, communication foibles, or cost overruns. In fact, these leaders provide the kind of attention to practical details that is rarely found in the activity of other types of leaders. It is the operational leader who often bears the bad financial news but is rarely responsible for the actions that produced such difficulties.

By working on operational details every day, the operational leader sometimes loses sight of the fact that he or she is to be a leader, not a manager. That role confusion can cause the leader to behave more like a manager and lose sight of the vision in favor of simply running a well-oiled machine—regardless of where it is headed. Such confusion can obviously hurt the ministry since it is the operational leader whose attention to detail often provides the financial, administrative, or systemic correctives that facilitate ministry impact. Operational leaders, by nature, dislike conflict and will sometimes give in easily in situations where a tough stand might result in an emotional battle. At other times the "manager" in these people may cause them to make choices that produce short-term results at the long-term expense of the ministry.

COMPLEMENTARY, NOT COMFORTABLE

Can you understand how teaming these four types of leaders together would give rise to a dynamic, multifaceted hub of authority? And do you see now why few leaders possess more than one of these aptitudes?

> *Being with people who are just like us*
> *may feel more comfortable and appropriate, but invariably*
> *it leads to distress and disaster.*

A big mistake churches often make is teaming leaders who have the same aptitudes rather than complementary aptitudes. Why would we do that? Because we're human. Being with people who are just like us may feel more comfortable and appropriate, but invariably it leads to distress and disaster. Working intimately with people of divergent skills and views may make us less comfortable, but it invariably produces better results. Effective leadership teams almost always have a degree of creative tension because they are composed of people who approach the same problem differently. That creative tension is simply one of the positive building blocks that propels a well-matched team forward; remove the tension and you eliminate one of the strengths of the team.

Given the description of the four leadership aptitudes provided above, consider the dynamics of having four *directing leaders* trying to work together on the same team. They all love the pressure of making tough calls, their position in the public eye as they communicate the vision and direction, and the challenge of solving a vexing problem. But get them together and you'll need to take cover, because heated words and heavy objects will start flying when it comes time to make decisions or gain the attention of the public they serve!

What about bringing together multiple *strategic leaders?* Although they are less high-profile than the directing leaders, strategic leaders also make for a toxic mix when combined. You can expect great documentation, insightful analysis, and terrific planning, but don't hold your breath waiting for the congregation to willingly follow this group. Also realize that the plans might be sharp and well communicated, but they are not likely to be embraced because the people don't trust this quartet. They are not likely to exhibit the people skills required to build a strong coalition around their clever plans.

If it's people skills you want, then why not enlist the services of a quartet of *team-building leaders?* Get four of these leaders together and they will provide you with a world-class lovefest. Congregants will look forward to the fun-filled, high-connection gatherings they pull off. You might see some resources produced—telephone directories, new Rolodex cards, a calendar of future events—but don't count on much progress toward the vision.

Blending a handful of *operational leaders* would result in a tidy, efficient meeting with a carefully designed process—but without the heart or inspiration needed to stimulate followers to jump into the fray. People would know what they are expected to do; they would understand the details involved in carrying out their job;

there would be ample assessment and progress reports; but after a while congregants would lose sight of the big picture and simply feel like they were part of a well-oiled machine that is in maintenance mode.

Merely piecing together a group of warm bodies who are capable of working together—even if they agree on specific outcomes—is not likely to produce optimal results. Teams work best when they are comprised of individuals whose personal abilities and gifts contribute value while their personal deficiencies are compensated for via the abilities and efforts of other team members.

TEAMS CAN BE FRAGILE

We have to be realistic about this, of course. While teaming these four leadership aptitudes may produce incredible results, it also facilitates dynamic tension and occasional conflict. That tension will never disappear because each leader type has a unique perspective on leadership and the vision—and also brings divergent skills, thinking styles, and contextual perspectives to the table. If that tension can be properly managed, it is one of the sparks that keeps the team growing, innovating, and charging forward.

Consider one other crucial insight: *If the team is lacking one or more of these leader types, it is missing a necessary component in its efforts to facilitate transformation.* While no one of these leaders is more important than any other (although we typically praise the directing leader and take the others for granted), none can be successful without the partnership of the other types. As you reflect on the implications of this, keep in mind that this division of skills, focus, and energy explains why so many solo leaders feel overwhelmed, burned out, and incapable of leading effectively.

The key to effective team leadership, then, is having multiple leaders with *complementary* aptitudes working together, regardless of the size of the church or the nature of the ministry they are leading. Leadership teams that have these four types working cooperatively are needed to lead not just the entire church, but also the departments and programs within the ministry—and that means identifying a wealth of leaders to integrate into the leadership process.[1]

TEAM DYNAMICS

If you have ever tried working in a team environment, then you know that it is more complex than simply throwing four gifted leaders with complementary talents together and expecting them to create synergistic results. Just as a family produces group dynamics that must be understood and strategically managed, so must a leadership team be comprised of individuals who are willing to work hard at making the team a healthy unit.

In practice, one of the most important attributes of an effective team leader is the commitment to serve not only the church but the other leaders as well. This invariably requires a willingness to sacrifice personal rewards and resources for the good of the team and the accomplishment of its goals. An individual who approaches the team as a platform for personal accomplishment is not likely to add value to the ministry. An individual who views the team as a means of maximizing his or her personal contribution will undoubtedly prove to be an asset—as long as that view is not based on using the team as a steppingstone to personal notoriety.

Teams also need partners who respect and believe in one another. Without a firm conviction that the leadership partners can be trusted to make good decisions, protect one another's best interests, and remain focused on the vision rather than personal glory, the team will go nowhere—regardless of how gifted and experienced each of the members may be. Leaders take risks. It is difficult to pursue risks if you do not trust the motives or abilities of others to make appropriate choices or to provide support. If a deep level of trust does not exist, team members are not likely to rely upon one another's judgment or capabilities when key moments arise.

Team members must be committed to increasing their expertise within the domain that they represent in the team mix. This means a commitment to constant learning through reading, classes, being mentored, case studies, and other means. If one member slacks off, the entire team suffers. An obligation of leadership is to take your responsibility seriously and to support your colleagues by pulling your weight. Personal growth in leadership thus becomes a lifelong challenge.

NOT EVERYONE IS A LEADER

For the sake of clarity, let me point out that most church people will not participate in ministry leadership. This is because most people are not leaders. Our research suggests that more than four out of every five believers are primarily followers. Naturally, everyone provides leadership in certain situations, but by inclination and gifting most people are followers who need to be led. They can contribute to the cause of Christ by using other gifts and skills. People who are leaders are neither better nor worse than followers; all of us have a significant role to play in the unfolding of the kingdom, no matter what that role may be. As Paul wrote:

> Just as each of us has one body with many members, and these members do not all have the same function, so in Christ we who are many form one body, and each member belongs to all the others. We have different gifts, according to the grace given us. (Romans 12:4-6)

Be careful not to assume that everyone who purports to be a leader is telling the truth. Our surveys find that most people—roughly three out of five adults and an even greater proportion of teenagers—claim that they are leaders. That, of course, is a gross overestimation. We learned that people like the image of being a leader but not the responsibilities, the constant criticism, and the hard work involved in leading. Most people do not have the wisdom and discernment, or the courage, to consistently make wise, strategic, tough choices, and to stand by those choices.

In the end, an effective leadership team is comprised of people who sacrifice their own notoriety and power because they believe they have been called to serve as leaders, because they are demonstrating godly character, and because they want to blend their skills and abilities with those who can add value to the mix. In great teams each partner makes a significant and necessary contribution to the end result. Because each person pulls his or her own weight in the relationship, there is a sense of interdependence, equality, and mutual respect that fortifies the determination of the group to overcome the odds and make the vision real.

CHAPTER SEVEN

"BEST PRACTICES" OF SUCCESSFUL TEAM LEADERSHIP

Great outcomes do not happen by chance.

When you watch a great organization at work, everything looks easy. The mission and vision of the organization are clear and attractive, the people seem to gladly and effortlessly fulfill their responsibilities, and impressive results appear to emerge on cue. Having worked with Fortune 500 companies, government agencies, political campaigns, nonprofit organizations, churches, and parachurch ministries, I have been privileged to glimpse behind the curtain at what it really takes for such results to occur.

As you might imagine, great outcomes do not happen by chance. Inevitably, there is a sophisticated, intentional, and strategic process propelling the organization forward.

To conduct research for this book we dug beneath the surface of several dozen churches across the country where effective lay-leadership teams are in place. Unfortunately, there was no standard formula and no magic process that works across the board. In fact, no two churches had identical processes for developing their team system—even their underlying philosophies of leadership and lay participation showed noteworthy variances. But we were able to identify a substantial and significant group of common practices—"best practices," if you will—that enabled these churches to emerge from the pack.

> *Leaders serving in these churches get great pleasure and satisfaction from leading within a team context.*

It is worth noting that our research even uncovered a trio of expected but important observations about the team-leadership process. First, leaders serving in these churches get great pleasure and satisfaction from leading within a team context. Second, the churches have a measurably broader ministry impact than do churches that do not utilize lay-leadership teams. Third, their potential for continued numerical growth is virtually unlimited—and the churches we studied are, in fact, exploding with numerical growth.

We found that the best practices of these churches fall into four general categories:

1. There are specific ways in which they create a viable leadership partnership.

2. They develop an environment designed to facilitate effective team leadership.

3. The ways in which the leaders perform their duties reflect some similarities.

4. Lay leaders are intentionally equipped to succeed in their roles.

CREATING VIABLE LEADERSHIP PARTNERSHIPS

Since leadership is about people serving people, we should begin a discussion of the process by understanding how the "people component" operates in these churches. Without appropriate software (people), it doesn't matter how sophisticated your hardware (systems and resources) might be: Nothing will be produced.

Recruiting a Team

It all starts with appropriate team design. This involves determining the proper number of people to invite into leadership teams (usually no more than six), specifying the criteria by which individuals are invited to become team members, defining the roles of each participant, describing the relationship between lay leaders and pastoral staff, fixing the term of service for team members, conceptualizing the training regimen for leaders, and so forth. These might seem like irrelevant details, but addressing these issues early allows the church and its leaders to focus on the important issues once the system is triggered.

Great teams are the result of intelligent recruiting. Just as a basketball team becomes successful because its scouts and executives have carefully planned their draft choices and trades to accumulate a roster of talented players with complementary skills, so do successful churches recruit high-potential lay leaders with the intent of developing their talent and matching them with other, complementary leaders. They look for attributes that suggest the likelihood of leadership impact: a definable leadership aptitude, a teachable spirit, mature faith, passion for the vision, a servant's heart, and basic leadership competencies. Once these individuals have been identified and recruited, they must be strategically blended into a team in which their contribution will multiply the team's impact.

> *Churches that create ineffective teams tend to match people on the basis of personality, assuming that personality conflicts represent doom for a team.*

Our research uncovered an interesting distinction between churches that effectively match lay leaders and those that do not. The churches that create ineffective teams tend to match people on the basis of personality, assuming that personality conflicts represent doom for a team. By contrast, churches that succeed with lay teams consider personality to be of minimal importance. The criteria by which they match lay leaders is each member's passion for the same vision, followed by complementary leadership aptitudes then levels of experience in leadership. Only then does personality come under consideration.

It was rare to find that successful churches reject an otherwise viable match solely on the basis of personality. Why? "We're dealing with spiritually mature people here," explained the senior pastor of a church that has dozens of thriving lay-leadership teams—none of which were developed around personality traits and styles. "The key to success is that they are sold out to the vision and they have skills that fit together well. Sure, we have some dicey moments when some of these high-performance, on-edge personalities first get together, but we have never yet had a serious battle. The common ground is the vision and the desire to serve. If we can help our leaders focus on those things, they get over the personality stuff."

Facilitating Collaboration

Once the individuals have been joined into a team, churches encourage them to spend time coming together as a close-knit, single-minded service unit. My observation of the process underscores several common threads churches employ to facilitate collaboration. One thread is that of creating biblical community within the team. The team is positioned to provide personal identity, a sense of belonging to something meaningful, status or prestige, and relational intimacy with peers. Another thread is that of developing unity. No matter how heated the internal disagreements may become or how diverse the members' points of view might be, once the team emerges from behind closed doors, they embrace one unified view. A related thread is that the team arrives at a means of making cooperative decisions based on the diversity of talents, experiences, and gifts resident within the group. Yet another thread is that team members find the delicate balance between maintaining their personal independence and developing a satisfying dependence upon one another. All of these developments won't accomplish much unless there is genuine mutual respect among members.

In the churches we studied, the process of facilitating those outcomes varied considerably. Most churches, however, provided mentoring and oversight from a pastor during the initial stage of the group's life, then transferred the shepherding responsibility to the team captain within a short period. In fact, one of the factors often used in selecting team captains was their ability to help the team become a truly collaborative unit.

Signing a Covenant

Another key to successful team building was for the team to draw up a written covenant. Some agreements were simple, one-page commitments to serve God, team members, and the church in accordance with specified biblical principles and a standard of personal excellence. Others were multipage, detailed documents covering a broad array of practices and perspectives that included the ministry vision, plans, goals, strategies, standards of behavior, methods of accountability, penalties for failure to live up to the agreement, member tenure, and specific personal spiritual growth needs and commitments.

At first it seemed to me that such documents took the whole

arrangement too far. But after studying the effect of these covenants, I realized their value. "When I signed that covenant," recalled one lay leader at a large Methodist church, "I really had to stop and think about what I was agreeing to do. There's something about putting your name on the dotted line that gives the agreement a real seriousness that seems more real than simply talking through some points of agreement and giving verbal assent." Many lay leaders admitted that they occasionally return to the covenant to study it, hoping that they have not failed to live up to their responsibilities.

A final aspect of creating the lay-leader partnership is choosing a captain for the team. Once again, this may seem like a minor detail hardly worth mentioning, but it turns out to be a highly significant task that can make or break the health and impact of the team. In fact, it is so important that I will devote the entire next chapter to the process of selecting the team captain.

Developing a Friendly Environment

A team's success is somewhat dependent on the environment provided for leadership. While we witnessed some cases in which teams succeeded despite a hostile environment, the more common observation was that churches that dared teams to overcome the environment rarely had healthy and effective teams in place. The wisest strategy is for a church to intentionally clear the path for teams so that they have the greatest opportunity to experience success.

Setting teams up for victory means that there must be a culture that supports lay-leadership teams. There are numerous examples of cultural conditioning for team impact, such as expecting all leadership to be conducted by teams, encouraging laity to assume key leadership posts, and deferring decisions until the appropriate team has made a choice. Symbols of the importance of teams include the titles given to team-based leaders ("lay minister," "ministry director," and "lay pastor" are examples), requiring leadership teams to develop the church budget (rather than having pastoral staff make those determinations), and taking time in corporate events, such as worship services and congregational meetings, to introduce the congregation to each team and its members.

Many churches had revised their values statements to reflect the significance of the team approach. For instance, some of the values specified included the notions that key ministry decisions are to be made by lay-leadership teams, that team leadership is esteemed more highly than solo leadership, and that the church is responsible for preparing team leaders for positive experiences. Some churches rewrote their constitutions to describe their decision-making process as team based; others introduced program development and accountability systems based on teams conceiving, implementing, and evaluating such ministry efforts. All of these instances were designed to communicate an inescapable truth: Our church lives and dies by its lay-leadership teams.

The External Context

Preparing the internal context (that is, the church culture) represents only one side of the coin. The other side relates to the external context—the world culture and its impact on the church's ministry. For the leadership teams to reach their potential, they must understand the challenges and opportunities in the world we have been called to inhabit and influence. Facilitating such analysis and interpretation in relation to the church's vision and strategic thrust will not only shape the choices of the ministry but also determine whether the teams will optimize their influence both inside and outside of the church.

A Significant Challenge

A team that thrives must coalesce around a significant challenge. Good leaders tend to be busy, intelligent, skilled, active people. Unless they have a serious challenge before them—and in the case of team-based leadership, one that clearly transcends the ability of each individual member, working alone, to meet the challenge— the team will never rise to its loftiest potential. Leaders' adrenaline pumps when it seems that a challenge is impossible to overcome. The team truly revs up to full gear when there is a sense of urgency added to the magnitude of the challenge.

Behavior and Accountability

Every great team holds itself accountable to standards of behavior as well as performance goals. The evaluation process is handled as objectively as possible, often involving the help of an outsider (such as a staff member) familiar with the work of the group, and is designed to reflect the highest levels of integrity. Great teams know that you only improve what you can measure and that you should bother to measure only that which is meaningful in light of your vision.

It was interesting to learn that the teams we observed did not carry out such accountability once a year, as if conducting an annual job performance for an employee. Rather, the teams we watched were constantly asking themselves tough questions about all levels of team activity—questions related to quality, strategy, community, pace, passion, image, productivity, stewardship, and so forth. How pleasing it was to recognize that this self-accountability process had quickly become second nature to these teams in short order. And the process cuts two ways. First, they evaluate the team itself, and second, they regularly evaluate one another as contributors to the team effort. This determination to do the right things right was refreshing and challenging.

Enabling High-Level Performance

For great leadership to transpire, the team must engage in specific activities. For instance, we found that highly effective teams work hard to facilitate outstanding communication. Sometimes the relationships and information flow occur naturally, but often the team must focus on intentionally enabling good communication to happen. One aspect of this art is to ensure that the team has frequent times for interaction, whether via scheduled meetings or telephone appointments or other tools such as e-mail. Encouraging team members to listen carefully to what one another has to say is another tactic that we saw enforced.

An outcome of the team's emphasis upon community and collaboration is the development of an environment in which everyone is expected to contribute useful insights. Openness to everyone's input is critical to fostering understanding and excellence as well as the sense that each person adds value to the team. (As will be discussed in the next chapter, the captain is frequently the individual who made sure that the communication process was healthy within the team.)

Measured Risks

A team that is afraid to take risks is a team that will not serve its constituency well. Leadership is about making choices, and always taking the safest route will limit the potential of the team's ministry. Of course, a team should not be reckless in its decision making, but neither should it limit its ministry potential because it is scared to try something and fail. The best teams are those that take measured risks. If the risk does not pay off, they learn from those failures so that future decisions will be more productive. When a team lacks reasonable caution or consistently makes inadvisable choices, then it may be time for the group's overseer (often the pastor or a staff person) to provide tighter guidance on its operations. The overseer may need to portray the recent decisions as failures, clearly define the objectives and standards by which the team should operate, or change either the captain or the team members in order to raise the performance level of the group.

Disciplined, Narrow Focus

Successful teams are disciplined. That means they have a narrow focus. In many churches where teams exist but are ineffective, a major reason is that they are expected to lead in areas that extend well beyond the boundaries of their charter or expertise. Great teams are not the savior of the church; they have a narrow, well-defined focus and stick to their niche. One of the captain's greatest contributions to the team is to help it say no to great opportunities, simply because those opportunities will divert the team's attention and resources from the very outcomes it exists to produce.

For example, a team that exists to lead the worship function within a church would be ill-advised to also step into a troubled Christian education program and try to solve its problems. Some observers will argue that this is foolish—that a strong team should serve wherever its services are needed and that people can handle more than one task at a time. Logical as that may sound, the track record of teams shows that they are effective when they zero in on one major challenge at a time, one in which they share a common vision and passion.

These are not teams built on a business model that implores the team to take whatever work it can get to generate revenue; they are based on a passion model that expects team members to exploit their gifts, abilities, and experiences to empower the church within a dimension of ministry about which the team members are passionate. Focusing on multiple areas of ministry will likely dissipate their time, resources, and skills, causing them to produce less-effective outcomes in the area of their primary calling as well as in the new area that they have taken on.

One interesting observation was that some team-driven churches have tried to bridge the gap between narrow focus and broad needs by creating one or a handful of "consultant" teams. The primary function of these teams is to step in to help fix daunting problems or address unusual challenges in a range of ministry areas within the church. The passion of the leaders in those teams is to provide help where help is needed in order to raise the ministry to its highest level. When a church has leaders who are willing to lead in this type of as-needed role and to devote themselves to learning whatever is needed to provide excellence within a variety of functions, this tactic can work well.

But no matter what the focus of a team is, success requires flexibility in the team's efforts. Because effective teams monitor their progress as they serve, there are constant midcourse adjustments being made. Rigidity undermines leadership. Because we lead people in dynamic environments, continual learning and recalibration are crucial to getting the job done with efficiency, impact, and excellence.

Shared Responsibility

High performance happens within the team when everyone shares the responsibility and makes significant contributions. You can tell if a team shares responsibility by its approach to problem solving. If the conversations regarding solutions become one-person dialogues regarding appropriate action to take, chances are good that the coalition is a work group rather than a team—that is, a collection of subordinates who dutifully and mindlessly take their orders from a chief. Great teams rely upon each person to lend his or her experience and expertise in developing creative and viable solutions to each challenge they face. If even one of the team members is frozen out of that chain of interaction, the entire team is crippled.

Measurable Goals

Measurable goals are among the most important components of a team's success. Goals focus the team on what is important while also giving the group a benchmark against which to compare its productivity and impact. Teams that meet their goals have reason to celebrate and set their sights higher. Teams that fail to reach their goals automatically receive a sense of their weaknesses and may then apply their problem-solving skills to their internal operations. We did note that teams lacking measurable goals also lack the same level of energy and focus that is evident within goal-driven teams.

> *If even one of the team members is frozen out*
> *of that chain of interaction, the entire team is crippled.*

God at the Center

A final factor critical to the health and impact of leadership teams is that of keeping God at the center of all things. Every great team we studied prays together regularly, and individual members pray daily about the team's responsibilities and performance. This emphasis on prayer is one of the indications of how seriously team members take their involvement in ministry leadership. Beyond prayer, we also found that effective teams lean heavily on the Bible for guidance, solutions, and behavioral parameters for the team.

Equipping Leaders for Impact

Every one of the churches we examined that uses teams to great effect provides leadership training on a regular basis. In some cases this constitutes a weekly, one-hour meeting in which there is time for teaching, dialogue, reporting, and relationship building. In other churches the process takes place monthly or quarterly. The most common strategy is to hold a monthly leadership-development event, scheduled for the same duration at the same time each month (for example, from 9 A.M. to noon on the third Saturday of every month).

Because these churches recognize that leaders learn from many experiences and in a variety of ways, developmental efforts are broad-based. Each church creates its own unique means of helping leaders grow, but we found two common principles among them:

First, they do not limit their training to lectures in a classroom. In most of these churches, the expert divulging useful information was involved intensively at the start of the leadership-training process, then more sparingly once leadership teams were in full gear. In other words, when an individual initially joins the leadership family at the church, there is often an intensive introductory training regimen that utilizes the lecture approach, but once that orientation process is completed, the training process is more interactive and individualized. Churches contextualize the training to account for the unique conditions and opportunities that define the church's ministry.

Second, these churches strive to elevate the performance of their leaders through a wide variety of training approaches. Even though many people have had extensive leadership training in the secular world, leading a business and leading a church are not the same. The same skills might be used, but it is imperative to differentiate some of the nuances such as the difference between a bottom-line mind-set and a servant mind-set.

METHODS OF ONGOING TRAINING

A typical team-driven church offers leaders at least a half-dozen ways to learn during the course of the year, such as:

1. *Regular self-assessment* leading to a personal growth plan. Because effectiveness demands a sense of quality, these churches expect leaders to measure themselves in key areas—character in particular, but competencies and outcomes too—and to pinpoint areas of strength and weakness. Great leaders maximize their strengths but recognize and attack their weaknesses to expand their capacity. Standardized tools may be used in this process such as spiritual gifts tests, leadership inventories, or church evaluation profiles, with special attention devoted to the areas in which the individual is providing focused leadership.

2. Many churches provide a *mentoring or coaching program* for all of their leaders. One approach is for the pastor

and other staff members to serve as "master mentors," with some of the mature lay leaders coaching less experienced lay leaders. This apprenticeship model is one of the most effective methods of expanding the numbers of leaders available to the church, while fortifying the ability to pass on the ministry's culture and strategies with a minimum of effort.

3. *Formal, classroom-style instruction* on leadership is almost universal—although most churches strive to make their classroom experiences into times of facilitated discussion rather than note-taking lectures. These meetings regularly bring leaders back to the basics—for example, the church's mission, vision, and values—and provide information on methods and perspective.

4. *Agendaless events*—described by one leader as "purposeful social events"—are designed to facilitate dialogue among leaders. While clergy are typically overworked, lay leaders are also busy people, generally juggling their occupation, family, and church responsibilities. There may be few, nonaccidental opportunities for lay leaders to interact with all of the other leaders in the church without an oppressive agenda hovering over their heads. Providing team members the chance to find out what other teams are doing, experiencing, and learning as well as the opportunity to maintain personal connections

often produces unpredictable but invaluable results for the ministry. Since leaders are problem solvers, these occasional connections with other leaders stimulate creative thinking and cross-team solutions that otherwise might not occur.

5. Many churches try to *keep their leaders up to date* on the latest and most helpful leadership resources. Some churches accomplish this by identifying useful resources for leaders and leaving it up to the individuals to pursue the resource if and when their time and interest allow that kind of follow-up. In other cases the church carves time out of regularly scheduled leadership meetings to call attention to key resources and to summarize one or more valuable lessons that can be drawn from the resource. Some churches go so far as to acquire and distribute the book, tape, or article in question to each leader, instructing him or her to digest the information and share some thoughts about it at a future leaders' meeting. The underlying desire, regardless of the approach, is to motivate church leaders to stay fresh and current in their thinking about leadership.

6. *Experience-based learning* has proven to have impressive influence in people's lives. Whether it be a "ropes course," some other type of adventure-based team-building experience, or any real-world experience that

conveys leadership lessons through hands-on participation, the more progressive (and larger) churches have recently begun focusing more attention on this means of development.

7. *"Road trips rule!"* Such was the exuberant exclamation of one young leader. He noted that he learns more from attending seminars and conferences in the company of fellow leaders and discussing the insights delivered in those events with his peers than from any other developmental process. He is not alone in that sentiment. Getting perspective from high-caliber, external experts can be a challenging and invigorating experience. The landscape is filled with ministry-oriented training events to choose from. Team-based churches often have a budget for taking a number of leaders to such events. One of the newest twists on this approach is the use of satellite-delivered training through which respected leaders broadcast their insights to a large number of churches (that is, downlink sites) so that leaders from all over the country—even from around the globe—can participate in the live event.[1]

One important view held by team-led churches—and verified by team members themselves—is that it is crucial to provide ongoing training and experiences for leaders to stay challenged, growing, and sharp. In spite of their busy lives, a majority of lay leaders we interviewed said that they wanted more training in leadership competencies and that they wanted that training to come from their church. This underscores the concept of the senior pastor as a leader of leaders rather than striving to be the dominant spiritual leader in the life of every congregant.

> *A majority of lay leaders we interviewed said that they wanted more training in leadership competencies.*

One of the ancillary benefits of providing regular training for lay leaders is that it reinforces the people's commitment to serving the church through leadership. Always keep in mind that as satisfying as leadership may be to those who practice this art within the church, lay leaders are under enormous pressure at work, at home, and in their personal relationships. Leadership, by its very nature, is difficult; a church cannot afford to take these people for granted. Like any human being trying to make his or her life count, leaders can get discouraged. They need to be loved and appreciated. Continual, quality training is one way to recognize their contribution, celebrate their victories, and reinforce their participation as leaders.

THE MARKS OF SUCCESS

What happens when a church has effective teams leading the way? People's lives are changed. Increasing numbers of individuals become more Christlike in various ways. This is the primary function of leaders: to see people's lives transformed in conjunction with the vision for change that the Lord has conveyed to the church. It is only natural that the primary point of assessment would relate to life change.

Great teamwork also produces a church that enjoys rich community. Ministry is about people and their relationships with God and one another. Effective leadership enables people to enjoy deeper and more enriching interaction. Naturally, another outcome is that the goals set by the team are accomplished—some of which will relate specifically to transformation and relationships, but others may be more narrowly focused.

Another result to look for is evidence of continual self-evaluation at the individual, team, and congregational levels. The church that does not constantly assess how it is doing is a church that will seduce itself into believing that affirmative anecdotes and self-generated praise represent reality. Effective team-led churches know better than to fall into that trap, and they will constantly search for ways to improve their strategies and outcomes.

CHAPTER EIGHT

THE CAPTAIN: THE TEAM'S POINT PERSON

---

*The selection of the captain
can make or break the team.*

On sports teams the position of captain is often ceremonial, a post awarded to the team's star performer or to someone who has served the team well for many years. Often that role comes with limited responsibility, such as leading the team out of the locker room, representing the team during the pregame coin toss, and conveying referees' decisions to the rest of the team.

In business and ministry, however, where the fate of the organization is dependent upon the quality of the leadership provided, the role of the team captain is far from an empty commendation. While a top-flight captain does not make the entire team great, a mediocre captain can hinder the performance of an otherwise effective team. Thus the selection of the captain often makes or breaks the team.

One of the more surprising outcomes of our research into

effective lay-leadership teams was that every successful team we observed had a captain in place. Their jobs were far more than ceremonial, high above simply calling meetings and arriving early to make sure the coffee was ready. Captains proved to be the pivot on which the teams revolved.

WHY A TEAM NEEDS A CAPTAIN

Perhaps it seems that having a captain on a team of leaders unnecessarily invites dissension. Will selecting one person to oversee the energies of the team be unhappily interpreted by the others as singling out the captain as the best leader or the most important person in the group?

On the contrary, our exploration of leadership teams showed that the role of the captain was accepted as necessary by team members—if the role was properly described and positioned. In essence, the captain is the facilitator of the team's process. As a team becomes busy doing its work, someone must serve as the traffic cop to ensure that necessary efforts are neither overlooked nor hindered by unproductive or inappropriate group dynamics.

FIVE WAYS THE CAPTAIN LEADS THE TEAM

How does a captain capably perform this duty of keeping the team focused, productive, and mutually supportive without derailing his or her own unique leadership contribution to the common cause? This individual must have the ability to balance two unique roles:

(1) the specialization he or she provides in the leadership mix (for example, representing one of the four leadership aptitudes), and (2) the function of a process facilitator. To faithfully carry out this dual role, the captain juggles leadership within the ministry focus and the ministry to fellow leaders.

1. The Captain Maintains the Team's Focus on the Vision

Someone must attach blinders to the vision of the team so that it will stay focused. Chances are there will be numerous opportunities to accomplish positive, tangible outcomes along the way that have nothing to do with the vision around which the team was brought together—and which actually deter from the unique mission to which the team is called. The captain is responsible for keeping the team aligned with its vision day after day, identifying alluring alternatives as distractions from the true goal of the team. The captain may not be the main vision-caster of the group, but he or she ought to be the primary champion of the vision within the group. If a team loses sight of its reason for existence, the captain has failed the team and the team will fail the church.

> *The captain is responsible for keeping the team aligned with its vision day after day.*

2. The Captain Facilitates Positive and Productive Relationships Among Team Members

A team must move together in harmony if it is to reach its goals. Such progress demands good relationships among the members.

Yet the aggressive, strong-willed, independent nature of most leaders can result in tenuous interaction unless someone assumes the role of negotiator among them. A great captain maintains a good working relationship with each member, senses impending relational danger, and proactively helps the team to avoid counterproductive engagements. Captains empower members to provide their views and add to the team mix without feeling that they are being overpowered by others.

3. The Captain Identifies Opportunities for Individual Growth

Ideally, each team member is continually in the process of becoming a better leader and disciple. The captain powers that developmental emphasis by encouraging efforts to grow, by recognizing growth that is evident, by identifying specific aspects of a leader's character or competencies that require improvement, and by informing a leader of upcoming opportunities for useful training or education. This might entail alerting a team member to classes, noting new resources that are available, or discussing personal leadership weaknesses that the individual needs to address. The ultimate goal for the captain is to motivate each team member to grow as a leader and as a follower of Christ.

4. The Captain Prepares the Team to Move Ahead by Acquiring Resources

A team without resources will not get far. The captain strives to pave the way toward progress by generating the resources necessary for sustained movement by the team. This might entail human resources, financial resources, or other components needed to move the team's ministry closer to fulfilling its vision. A captain must therefore stay well informed of what each team member will be doing in relation to the team's ends and anticipate the resources required to produce the intended outcomes.

5. The Captain Demonstrates Personal Leadership Productivity

Accepting the position of captain does not exempt the individual from carrying his or her own weight within the team's activity. To maintain the respect of team members as well as the balance of skills and competencies within the group, the captain must continue to do the work and produce the outcomes expected by the rest of the team. Failure to keep up will undermine the captain's standing. In the eyes of team members, the captain is a team member first, a captain second.

IMPORTANT CONSIDERATIONS

Can a team operate effectively without a captain? Yes, but not without someone's filling the captain's role anyway. In some ministries an outside ministry professional—such as a pastor or staff member—serves as a surrogate captain. This approach, however, usually prevents the team from operating at peak effectiveness because the outsider has neither a complete understanding of the team's activity and temperament nor the complete trust of the team members. While an outside captain is often better than no captain, the ideal is to have a team member pull double duty—

serving both as a productive group member as well as the team's captain. Further, I often have seen that when a church uses a pastor or paid staff person in the captain's position, an underlying reason is to preserve control over what the team is doing—and this can be more debilitating than operating without a captain.

Which leadership aptitude works best in the captain's role? While *directing leaders* usually assume that they should be the team's leader, they often make terrible captains because of their lack of detail orientation and their insensitivity to the quirks of other members. *Strategic leaders* are good with details but generally lack the people skills to serve effectively in this role. *Team-building leaders* provide the interpersonal encouragement that is often needed to complement the delivery of bad news but often lack the focus on specifics and the commitment to plans that shape effective team development. In the end, you may discover *operational leaders* are your best bet for captain, especially since they typically are process oriented and the captain's position is a process role.

THE MAKING OF A GREAT CAPTAIN

Leaders may be born, but captains are appointed and refined. No matter how an individual assumes the captaincy, there are certain functions that make a person shine in this role.

A person is not likely to perform the job well unless he or she understands the captain's role. Simply put, *that role is to be the chief servant of the team.* In addition to facilitating outcomes and group health, the captain always has an eye on how to build up the team members and the team itself. In the churches we studied, the individual who served as coach or overseer of the team—usually a pastor or staff person—often invested additional time and energy mentoring the captain as to the nature of the captain's role. This investment was heaviest in the early life of the group and during the formative months of the captain's tenure.

Leaders may be born,
but captains are appointed and refined.

Great captains never trumpet their position as captain. The captain simply accepts the added responsibilities as one way in which to help ensure the success of the team as it pursues God's vision. A great captain is one who blends in with the others, always remembering that the team is the hero—not an individual in the group—and that the team retains control in each situation. Being effective in the role of captain demands a sensitive balance between providing guidance or control—determining how far to go, how strong to be, or how much to back off.

To faithfully execute the role of captain, the individual must wholeheartedly believe in the people on the team and in the vision they are pursuing. Anything less than complete trust in and respect for the team members will result in favoritism and an innate unwillingness to provide total support to each member equally and unequivocally. Failure of the captain to "own" the vision will undermine his or her commitment to the team members, the team process, and ministry outcomes.

In many respects leadership teams are similar to marriages in that they demand time to foster a deep relationship among the partners, a unity of perspective, and the furtherance and protection of mutual best interests. Research on divorce emphasizes that poor communication is one of the major reasons why marriages falter; on teams, captains can maximize the chance for success by facilitating the communication process. Effective captains listen carefully, constantly, and completely—keeping the flow of communication consistent, hearing what is not being said as well as what is said, and clarifying the content of messages conveyed. While all leaders need to be good communicators to be effective, there is a tendency among leaders to tell others what to do or how to do it without listening to what the others are saying. A team captain must remain vigilant against this kind of one-sided communication that can only destroy relationships.

Captains also serve the team by encouraging the group to push to its highest level of performance and productivity. Without someone on the inside standing guard against any slippage of standards, the chances are good that leaders will do what it takes to merely get by and move on. Great captains push their teams to live up to the highest performance standards without lowering the bar when things get tough.

Along the way, great captains encourage their teams to take plausible risks. A team that does not risk will not lead people very far. The natural tendency of teams—especially those that are newly formed or are seeking to make their mark in ministry—is to follow the safe path and accept whatever progress can be achieved without risking failure. Great captains motivate the team to push themselves to the point of maximum output. Sometimes the results will catapult the ministry forward; other times, even an all-out effort results in failure. Captains, however, can help their teams use failure as a step toward success, dissecting the undesirable results to learn insights that will serve the team as it takes new ground in future forays.

In the end, a valuable captain is like adding another member to the team without having to recruit, train, and integrate another person. The captain accepts the role with humility, fulfills the role with energy and wisdom, and enhances the team through servanthood. A great captain always remembers that the role is about the health of the team, not about his or her ascendancy to greater glory and reputation. The captain succeeds only when the team succeeds. No matter how competent and superbly he or she serves the team, if the team fails, the captain also fails. Such an all-for-one-and-one-for-all philosophy prohibits the team from blaming others for its shortcomings, offering excuses for its problems, or lowering its standards to accomplish results.

SELECTING THE CAPTAIN

One of the most counterintuitive lessons we learned from our exploration of leadership teams was how churches usually select their team captains. It seemed reasonable to expect the members of the team to assemble, assess themselves, and determine which of them the others would most like to follow.

To the contrary, we discovered that the process seems to work best when the captain is chosen for the team by an outside force—usually by the senior pastor or the staff person to whom the team reports. While this initially may seem like heavy-handed domination, this process works well if the individual who selects the captain truly comprehends the significance and the role of the position.

Let's assume that the pastor determines the captain. This makes sense because the pastor is likely the individual who brought the team together in the first place. Consequently, the pastor is most likely to know the relative strengths and weaknesses of each team member and which individual is best skilled to carry out the captain's role. In most cases the pastor has no greater motivation in selecting the captain than to see the team succeed—and therefore has a vested interest in appointing someone who will move the team forward most effectively.

When a team selects its own captain, politics are often at the heart of the process. Seeing the captain's position as a feather in one's cap rather than as a means of serving others, the team gets off on the wrong foot right at the start, competing for power and perks rather than cooperating for group performance. The team members probably do not know one another's strengths and weaknesses in the beginning, which only heightens the prospect of making an inappropriate choice of captain. In fact, few team members are likely to have a solid grasp of the captain's function and are therefore incapable of intelligently selecting the best team member for the job.

There's another good reason for an outsider to choose the captain: The team needs a captain early in its history, and that person needs to get off to a fast start. Since the team will take time to develop its own pace and inner equilibrium, it is invaluable to have a leader in place to foster that development and to help the team capitalize on what it is learning. A captain who can make the most of those early developments will win the loyalty and trust of the team, but a captain who is ignorant of that growth or misinterprets the lessons will never gain the team's confidence. Having had some history with each team member, the pastor or staff person is more likely to identify the person who will quickly and accurately absorb the lessons emerging from the team's initial experiences.

Unfortunately, there are numerous churches in which captains are selected by pastors or staff for the wrong reasons—usually to maintain control. By installing a captain who will serve the needs, interests, or demands of the person who gave him the position, the selector increases the probability of being able to pull the strings of the puppet captain. This situation, of course, is unhealthy and merely reflects the dysfunctional nature of the church. An unhealthy connection between captain and selector often spawns an unhealthy team and leadership environment.

SIGNS OF A BAD CAPTAIN

Inevitably, no matter who makes the selection, there are times when a team is saddled with a bad captain. It is not a sign of failure or defeat to recognize a bad choice and replace him or her with a new leader, although that transition must be handled deftly. How do you know when you have a bad captain? Watch for these telltale signs:

- When there is *consistent dissension among team members,* the captain is failing to harmonize relationships satisfactorily. Sometimes the captain is busy balancing so many other activities that the griping has gone unnoticed. A simple, discreet observation about the situation made by the team's outside coach or supervisor may trigger the appropriate response. If a positive adjustment is not forthcoming, however, failure to squelch the disunity may result in irreparable damage.

- Some individuals *let the position go to their heads or misinterpret the intended role.* A captain who becomes overly controlling, making unilateral decisions instead of soliciting team input, is a sure sign of this cancer. When a captain interprets the position as the delivery of power, it is best to address that problem quickly. If the issue persists, a more radical response may be required.

- Listen to how team members and congregants describe a given team. *If a team becomes labeled "Bob's team" or "Jane's team,"* and you are able to trace the source of that label to Bob or Jane, then the captain has a misplaced understanding of his or her role. Naturally, in some situations outsiders will refer to the team by the name of its most public or competent member or by the name of its titular captain. More often, though, this problem stems from the behavior of the captain. When that individual fosters such an identity, or persists in taking credit for what the team has done, this form of personification is unwarranted and unacceptable.

- In some instances a *team begins to focus on its achievements rather than its vision.* Since one of the dominant roles of the captain is to keep members focused on the vision and to measure all achievements in light of the fulfillment of that vision, this weakness could well be a sign that the captain is ineffective or ill-informed regarding the captain's role.

- Great teams solve problems creatively. If you study the output of a team and notice that *its solutions are predictable, uninspired, or only moderately successful,* the captain may be the culprit. A great captain will not allow the team to accept the path of least resistance; a lazy or incompetent captain may not know the difference or may not think it matters.

- A team that is *mostly reactive instead of proactive* may lack inspired leadership from its captain. Teams that change lives are those that are on the lookout for new opportunities to bring people closer to God and to enhance their lives in Christ. That means the team is continually anticipating new options rather than waiting to respond to existing challenges.

- Talk to team members about how much they enjoy serving on their leadership team. If they exude enthusiasm and joy, the chances are good that their team captain has facilitated a positive leadership environment and is providing stellar support to each member. If *team members are dragging or seem duty-bound* rather than ecstatic, the captain is probably letting them down in terms of motivation and focus. Explore what the captain is doing to keep people's spirits high and their sense of impact fed. A captain who does not reinforce the efforts of his teammates is undermining their ability to persevere and to find the satisfaction that leaders should receive from their efforts.

- Do team members *complain of the duplication of efforts?* This may reflect lack of trust, inferior communication, bad planning, or inappropriate division of labor.

- *Sometimes captains are in over their heads.* This shortchanges the captain's position by minimizing the team's processing time in favor of individual productivity. A common result is that everyone on the team works hard and produces individually, but the synergy is absent and the sense of camaraderie that defines true teams is missing.

The existence of one or two of these deficiencies does not necessarily mean that your captain is detrimental to the team. Every leader has his or her weaknesses, and the value of the team process is that such deficiencies may be compensated for by the complementary skills of other team members. In the same way, every team captain is human and possesses a variety of weaknesses, some more glaring and significant than others. Captains are not automatically disqualified by their imperfections; if they were, we would be stymied once again by the leader-as-superhero problem that team leadership is intended to solve. It is only when a captain's weaknesses significantly cripple or disable the team that it may be time to consider a change of internal leadership.

CHANGING CAPTAINS IN MIDSTREAM

When a change of captain is merited, the switch is usually called for and carried out by the team itself. While I did witness a few circumstances in which the pastor or church staff made the call, it is a sign of a healthy, growing team if it recognizes its own weakness and makes the appropriate changes to restore or improve its standing.

Perhaps the most significant aspect of replacing a captain is ensuring that the individual being replaced is not crushed in the process. In some cases, the departing captain is reassigned to another team, but unless the person's original passion for the vision his former team was pursuing has changed dramatically, this is a difficult change to justify. More commonly, the captain being replaced simply returns to his or her original leadership role (in alignment with a leadership aptitude) within the original team.

*Making too big a fuss over the transition
makes the change harder, while ignoring the transition
makes team relations awkward.*

The team's external coach (usually the pastor or staff liaison) may want to privately encourage each member to provide immediate acceptance of the new captain—along with genuine acceptance and affirmation of the replaced captain in his or her original role as noncaptain team member. Making too big a fuss over the transition makes the change harder, while ignoring the transition makes team relations awkward. The team's coach can help establish the right balance by reminding each member to be honest, sensitive, and supportive toward the former captain and to downplay the significance of the transition in favor of focusing more intently upon the team's current challenges and opportunities.

CHAPTER NINE

TRANSITIONING TO A TEAM-LED MINISTRY

*If the process is properly carried out,
the results will justify the effort.*

As we scoured the nation for examples of churches that effectively use lay-leadership teams, it became obvious that this approach to leadership is the exception to the rule. Even among the four out of ten churches that claim to be using leadership teams, a large majority actually have *work groups* led by an individual leader. Indeed, churches often confuse work groups (teams of gifted people serving under the direction of a gifted leader) with lay-leadership teams (teams of leaders working together).

One implication is that if churches are going to move toward lay-leadership teams, they will be making a dramatic transition from solo-based leadership to team-based leadership. That transition will tax the patience, resources, and will of the church. In the end, if the process is properly carried out, the results will justify the effort. But effectively making the shift demands a real commitment to lay-driven ministry, the releasing of leaders to truly lead, the redefining of the role of the pastor and staff, and the recognition and deployment of people's spiritual gifts and natural talents.

Let's discuss what it would take for a typical church to make the transition to being led by teams of lay leaders.

WHO LEADS THE CHANGE?

The initial impetus for a move to laity-based team leadership can come from anyone in the church—from the senior pastor to the newest member of the congregation. In effective churches, good ideas come from a wide spectrum of people and places, and the leaders of the church are wise enough and sufficiently open to consider those that have potential.

Once the idea of lay-team leadership is on the table, it is difficult to make the transition unless the senior pastor is supportive. The transition will redefine his or her role and will require that the pastor facilitate the switch to new ways of allocating power, distributing responsibility and resources, communicating with the congregation, and evaluating ministry outcomes. While it is theoretically possible for a church to make the transition in spite of the indifference or opposition of its senior pastor, that is likely to happen only if the pastor has very limited influence in the church's decision-making process and is not looked to by the congregation for behavioral and procedural cues. In most churches, even though the influence of the senior pastor is not what it used to be, the pastor remains the dominant agent of influence concerning the nature and direction of the church.

There is a difference between identifying the primary change agent and ensuring that key influencers on staff and among the congregation support the proposed change. We found many examples of churches where the pastor was ready to make the switch from solo leadership to team leadership but was ineffective at building the supportive coalition required to facilitate the move. In African-American churches, what the pastor says is usually accepted without question: Black congregations more readily accept moving from solo leadership to team leadership if the pastor promotes the shift. In Caucasian churches, though, a change of this magnitude may not even get a fair hearing among the congregation, no matter what the pastor desires. If the idea is proposed and backed by the senior pastor and finds initial favor among the people, then the key to success is whether the people trust their leaders to make good decisions and how effective those leaders are at mobilizing congregants around the details and implications of the transition.

In most churches, the scenario that has worked well begins with the senior pastor's embracing the idea, regardless of who introduced the possibility. How the pastor handles the idea will likely determine the fate of lay-leadership teams at the church.

Senior Pastor Is Key

If the church has a senior pastor working in conjunction with other ministry staff, then the pastor may fruitfully initiate the transition by building a strong team at the professional staff level. This is important because it sends the message that the pastor is serious about integrating this process into the life of the church and that he or she is skilled at facilitating that reality. Because people learn best by watching a model in action, providing the congregation with a working example of how teams operate is a powerful, valuable step in sparking the transition. If the church is small and has only the senior pastor as its professional ministry personnel, then the pastor must focus on treating core lay leaders as the people who will become the practical advocates of team-based lay leadership.

> *The pastor must become*
> *a champion of the change.*

Whether the church is large or small, the pastor must become a champion of the change to all who might be influenced by it. In addition to modeling teamwork and encouraging people to minister with a team mentality, this means that the pastor must strategically initiate the transition. It starts with preparing the congregation—intellectually, theologically, operationally, and emotionally—to make the change. This implies teaching about leadership and churchmanship from a team-driven perspective; repositioning people's notions of power, authority, responsibility, and influence; and getting people used to the notion that the pastor is no longer the primary leader of everything in the church but instead provides strategic leadership to core leaders.

People respond well to changes that promise greater value and benefit than sacrifice and suffering. But a constant in all leadership experience is that most people resist change, even when it is in their personal best interests. Jack Welch, the former CEO of General Electric, once brilliantly observed, "Change has no constituency." If you plan to make the change to team-based leadership, get ready for a fight. The breadth and intensity of the battle depends upon how well you prepare people for the shift in advance of initiating the transition and on how strategic you have been in aligning key leaders to support the move prior to going public with the idea.

CHANGING THE CHURCH CULTURE

Once the idea has been floated publicly, a series of foundations have to be put in place to increase the chances of a successful transition. The first and most far-reaching of those changes relates to the culture of your church.

Every church has a culture—its system of meaning and its ministry context. A culture is the cumulative body of symbols, traditions, values, acceptable behaviors, ideals, language, and customs that creates a unified way of life and a unique means of interpreting and experiencing reality. Your church's culture affects everything related to the ministry. If you want the transition to lay-led leadership teams, you must align the church's culture with the requirements and practices found in the team-based approach.

The shift in culture may entail a variety of new perspectives that congregants should adopt. For instance, one useful shift would be to alter the notion of leaders as *volunteers* to leaders as *lay ministers.* Along with such a change in perception and terminology would come a transition in the treatment of lay ministers from the status as *unpaid laborers* to that of *part-time ministry professionals*— still unpaid but regarded as equals in ministry. Repositioning various perspectives in this way will help facilitate the move from solo to team leadership.

Values for Successful Team Leadership

In addition, our observations suggest that the transition will fail unless a church's values are consistent with a team-based approach. Values are the principles and standards that define what is right, desirable, and worthwhile within the system. Your values, therefore, delineate your character as a ministry. But be aware that there are two types of values that churches possess: *stated values* and *latent values*. In the past decade it has become common for churches to fashion a values statement defining the values of the church. Common elements in those statements include integrity, personal holiness, humility, confession, servanthood, and so forth. Just as powerful and significant, however, are the latent values— principles and standards not written in an official church document but observable in the accepted or expected behavior and thinking of the church. Healthy congregations purposefully align their stated and latent values; when these are disjointed, politics replaces faith as the dominant focus of the church.

If you want to move to team-based leadership, then your values must promote such an environment and practice. Here are some of the items you might consider integrating into both your stated and latent core values:

- The church promotes the identification and application of *personal spiritual gifts,* used for the good of the worldwide church, the benefit of the local body of believers, and the joy and fulfillment of the individual in service to the kingdom of God (1 Corinthians 12:4-8).

- All of the church's ministry efforts are geared toward *promoting God's kingdom,* not individual agendas or splinter group priorities (Matthew 6:33).

- All work done by the church is to be done with *excellence,* with the realization that we are working for God, not for men or institutions (Colossians 3:23).

- The body of Christ is best served by *collaboration, not competition.* Whenever possible, congregants will work together toward a common outcome rather than vie for resources and commendations based on individual productivity (Matthew 20:20-28).

- The church reflects the unity of God when its leaders work in close-knit cooperation toward a commonly held vision from the Lord. Rather than seek leadership from individuals of extraordinary ability, this *church strives to build teams* of God-gifted believers combining their unique and complementary abilities toward the fulfillment of that vision. Teamwork focused on following God's will for the church is always supported more readily than isolated individual efforts (Acts 6:1-7).

- The health of this ministry is witnessed by *reliance upon multiple leaders* rather than upon the direction of a single leader. While the church esteems the senior pastor as the individual whom God has ordained to provide the ultimate direction to His people, the pastor succeeds by empowering the other leaders God has brought to the congregation to use their gifts and abilities in service to God and to the body of believers (Acts 15:1-22).

- This ministry is to be evaluated not only according to what it does but also according to how it ministers. In addition to the results we produce, we will also be *judged by the processes through which those outcomes are achieved.* The church does not accept the notion that God's vision will be pursued and fulfilled by the congregation "at any cost" since there are various methods, behaviors, and perspectives that may lead to desired results through inappropriate means (Revelation 3:1-3).

Your church's values charter may include a large number of values or a brief recitation of principles and standards. Regardless of the quantity involved, specifying those elements—and making them clearly known through teaching and application—is vital to a successful transition.

OTHER IMPORTANT DETAILS

Another key procedure in the early stages of the transition is for the transition team—that is, the senior pastor along with his or her confidants in bringing about this shift—to make sure that everyone has a clear and identical understanding of what is being contemplated and implemented.

One aspect of this process requires the clarification of language used in the transition. Terms commonly thrown about must be carefully defined and those definitions widely disseminated. Among the terms that ought to be clearly understood and embraced are those described in chapter 2: *leadership, leadership team, work groups, values, goals, vision, healthy ministry,* and *effective ministry.* It is also important to clarify the roles of key players whose lives will be affected in this transition, such as the senior pastor, elders, deacons, committee chairpersons, and church staff.

> *Terms commonly thrown about must be carefully defined and those definitions widely disseminated.*

Another set of helpful clarifications relates to key distinctions that will further people's understanding of the changes under consideration. For instance, do people know the difference between spiritual gifts and natural talents and the significance of each? Do they understand the different leadership aptitudes and how they fit together best? Is there a clear comprehension of the difference between trying hard and accomplishing good outcomes? Are congregants wise to the distinction between process and product and the implications related to these divergent but closely related elements?

In the early stage of the transition process, it is advisable to delineate the specific components of the team design that the church hopes to embrace. This means outlining details such as the ideal number of people to be incorporated into leadership teams; the specific roles leaders will play within those teams (for example, *directing, strategic, team-building, and operational, or some other useful designations*); the specific elements to be included in each team's charter or covenant; the process by which team members will be selected and invited onto a team; the dynamics of the lay leader–pastor–staff relationships; and the role of apprenticeships in the process.

A Plan of Action

Once the idea of moving to lay-leadership teams has been embraced by the primary change agent (usually the senior pastor) and the church's culture and the transitional details have been addressed, then it is time to develop a specific transition plan. While there is not one right way to formulate a plan, we did find certain elements that are common to successful action plans.

One of the most strategic commitments is to start small, iron out the inevitable miscues in the process, expand slowly, and eventually complete the transition with limited public fanfare. This low-key approach not only minimizes initial resistance but also builds congregational confidence in the process and in the team concept. Once there are a handful of lay-leader teams working smoothly and generating positive results, the congregation is likely to jump on the bandwagon: We may be living in an age of sophistication, but the old axiom, "Everybody loves a winner," remains as relevant today as ever.

This intimates that the initial team you select must be your best prospect for achieving success through team ministry. This team will be your experimental group and will have to endure hardships and challenges that future teams will not have to bear. The underlying notion is that if this, your best team, cannot make it, then there are other serious problems that need to be solved before the new paradigm is integrated throughout the church's ministry.

In the action plan for the transition, be sure to allow sufficient time for the experiment to produce as many insights as possible that will lead to a successful changeover. In some circumstances, speed is essential to success; however, when transitioning from solo-based leadership to team-based leadership, speed can be deadly. There is a slow learning curve that must be exploited to its fullest extent if the aggregate shift is to reap long-term benefits. Keep in mind that this is not just a change in the contours of leadership, but a redefinition of the very culture of the church. Allow for the time that such a grand transformation deserves.

Once the initial team has solidified and begun to operate efficiently, effectively, and consistently, you can use that initial triumph as a case study to persuade any skeptics in the congregation that the process is viable. It is best to be up-front about the lessons learned in the process and to describe how those hard-won insights will be incorporated into the development of additional teams.

> *When transitioning from solo-based leadership*
> *to team-based leadership, speed can be deadly.*

Macro-Level and Micro-Level Teams

In the action plan be sure to identify the foundational teams that the church will strive to create. This means differentiating between the macro-level and micro-level leadership teams to be created. Most lay-team-led churches have one *macro-level team* leading the aggregate ministry of the church; this team usually consists of several vocational and avocational individuals (for example, the senior pastor, a staff person, and two elders) whose combined gifts enable them to strategically lead the church. Then these churches are likely to have a variety of *micro-level teams*—groups of lay leaders who share the responsibility for directing the specific ministries within the church. For instance, there might be leadership teams for worship, evangelism, discipleship, stewardship, community, and community service ministry.[1] (Keep in mind that the leadership team does not necessarily consist of those individuals who will do the up-front work in that ministry, such as worship leaders who will play instruments and sing in the worship service. Team members are those who conceptualize, orchestrate, resource, facilitate, and evaluate the implementation of the music in the worship service.)

The macro-level leadership team will maintain the broadest view of the church's ministry, focusing upon the aggregate ministry efforts of the church and how those efforts relate to the church's vision. That team is responsible for keeping other teams as well as congregants focused on the grand vision of the church. In contrast, while each of the micro-level teams must be intimately acquainted with the church's overall vision and how their areas of ministry relate to that vision, they will most passionately pursue the component of the vision for which their team is primarily responsible.

Components of Your Action Plan
Your action plan should encompass:

- the identification of the micro-level teams

- a schedule for the introduction of each team into the life of the church

- the training and developmental resources required to facilitate the team leadership rollout

- the means of identifying potential leaders

- the leaders and management process by which the team rollout will be driven

- the transition from existing leadership groups (for example, elders, deacons) to leadership teams

- the methods to be used for resolving disputes that arise from the transition

- a way to handle questions that arise within the congregation about the transition

The action plan might also include information about how this entire process will be communicated to the congregation; how people who are not leaders will be integrated into the flow of ministry under the new approach; and an outline describing how leadership teams will interact with one another to coordinate the aggregate ministry of the church.

INTERNAL ACCOUNTABILITY

The success of your transition will ultimately depend upon how well the church prepares teams and team members to integrate a realistic accountability method into the leadership framework. Excellence happens only when performance standards are known and applied. Most people will live up to the expectations placed upon them if they believe they are going to be held accountable for their performance. The same principle seems to hold true for teams: Comprised of human beings, they will do as little as they have to in order to get by, but they will do whatever is necessary to avoid failing or to live up to the expectations they have agreed to uphold.

What should you hold leaders accountable for?

True leaders are qualified to lead because God has called them to that task (and has therefore gifted them for it) and because they have exhibited biblical character. Thus the primary focus for accountability among leaders is in the realm of character. Do they consistently and unerringly live in accordance with God's moral standards? A leader may prove to be incompetent and require training to raise his performance capacity, but that does not disqualify him or her from serving in leadership. Breaking God's moral code, however, represents a serious breach of trust and responsibility and may qualify as grounds for dismissal from the ranks of the church's leaders.

> *Excellence happens only when*
> *performance standards are known and applied.*

Leadership competencies—the functions that leaders undertake to motivate, mobilize, resource, and direct God's people in pursuit of His vision—are another area for which leaders should be held accountable. The purpose of this evaluative emphasis, however, is not so much to prove or disprove the worthiness of someone to lead as it is to identify the strengths and weaknesses of the leader so that he or she may improve personal levels of skill and leadership performance.

Leaders are responsible for facilitating ministry outcomes, so there must also be a degree of accountability for the results produced under their leadership. While many will rightly argue that God's greatest concern is with who we are rather than what we achieve, one of the distinctives of leaders is that they serve in order to facilitate life transformation within the body of believers. If such life transformation is not occurring, then we must question their capacity to lead. At the very least, the failure to produce positive spiritual outcomes may identify areas of personal development needed to enhance the individual's leadership.

Team leadership also requires some assessment of the quality of community fostered within each leadership collective. One of the keys to successful teamwork is the nature and depth of the relationships developed among team members. Examining the level of community among the members of a team is a telltale sign of their maturity and potential.

WHAT IF SOME TEAMS FAIL?

Sometimes even the most strategic and well-planned changes do not work out. What happens if one (or more) of the lay-leadership teams fail?

To address that question, we first have to define what we mean by team failure. We've identified seven chief ways in which any team might fail, and we strongly advise that you have a clear, proactive strategy in place to handle each type of failure should one occur. Let's look at the possibilities and determine what might be done in response to such failure.

First, a team could deteriorate due to the moral failure of one or more of its members. Experience shows that it is uncommon for multiple team members to experience moral failure simultaneously; usually, one member fails to live up to God's moral standards. The response to moral failure depends upon the culture of the church. Some churches believe that part of being in community is restoring a fallen member; others contend that because of the position of leaders, moral failure immediately disqualifies the individual from further leadership participation. In either case, you must also determine at what point a fallen leader is qualified to return to leadership responsibility.

Second, a team fails in its function if it reverts to solo-leadership practices. This defeats the reason for developing the team framework in the first place and undermines the church's investment of trust and resources in the team process. If reversion to solo leadership occurs, you must determine if the failure is systemic or related to the individuals on the team. The solution could be as simple as providing better definitions of team leadership or as dramatic as disbanding the team and replacing it with a new collection of leaders who are passionate about the same vision that had drawn the original team together.

Third, a team may fail to provide the initiative in ministry. Teams that wait passively for someone to point them in the right direction, tell them what to do, or identify existing problems or opportunities are of little use to the church. This is particularly true because team-based ministry demands cross-team integration—that is, multiple teams, each focused on a different dimension of the macro-level vision, working cooperatively. Often, working with the *directing leader* in the unit stimulates an appropriate improvement as this person is largely responsible for motivating the group to stay excited about the vision and to aggressively seek options for action.

Fourth, a team can fail to motivate the congregation to understand, own, and actively participate in the pursuit of the vision. If leaders, who are the primary champions of the vision, cannot get others excited about the vision, who will? Sometimes the failure is because team members are so enthusiastic about the possibilities that they try to fulfill the vision without involving outsiders. Other times the motivational skills of team members are not sufficient to generate congregational excitement and involvement. No matter what the underlying deficiency, getting the rest of the congregation to invest themselves in the totality of the ministry is imperative.

Fifth, sometimes the issue at stake is the inability to mobilize people around specific tasks in order to facilitate desired outcomes. While this may seem like a simple management function, the inability to organize people appropriately can dampen their enthusiasm for investing in the process. Occasionally you may find that the problem is miscommunication within the team (for example, the *directing leader* assumed the *team-building leader* would handle it, the *team-building leader* perceived this to be the job of the *operational leader,* and so forth). In other instances the issue is deeper: The leaders failed to think through how to efficiently identify and utilize the talents of the laity who demonstrate an interest in helping the team.

A sixth example of failure is attributable to not delivering the promised results. Leaders exist to serve people by helping them to achieve a specific outcome, as described by the team's vision. Whether the failure can be traced to a misunderstanding of the vision, a lack of adequate planning to generate desirable outcomes, the acceptance of inappropriate goals, effective methodology, or some other shortcoming, teams that do not produce results provide limited value to the ministry. People are leaders because they have the ability to identify specific outcomes and to produce those results. When leaders do not produce, they not only fail themselves and their team, but they let down the entire ministry they were called to serve. If that sounds harsh or overstated—many pastors protest when I describe this situation as evidence that leaders have failed—then you do not understand the responsibility that leaders shoulder when they accept their calling to lead. Merely trying hard or doing your best does not constitute effective leadership; it is provided by doing whatever it takes, within the boundaries of God's standards and people's capabilities, to deliver the results that do justice to the vision and also honor His calling to His church.

Seventh, a team fails when it leaves God out of the process. Effective teams pray constantly, always seeking the Lord's wisdom prior to any decisions they make. God's leaders always consider His principles and standards before moving ahead. The best leadership teams engage in serious spiritual development so that they have a deep and compelling relationship with the Lord whom they serve. Great teams always give the Lord the credit for the incredible things that happen as a result of their hard work and diligent efforts. If a team fails to integrate the ways of the Lord into their work, they become a mere business enterprise, using their abilities and resources to foster positive results. God expects more of His leaders than that. Anything less than a complete integration of God into the process and product of the team can be interpreted as failure.

> *God's leaders always consider His principles and standards before moving ahead.*

Most lay-leadership teams experience some type of failure in their life cycle. Such failure, however, need not be permanent or debilitating. Great teams recognize their failings and use them as a springboard to success. Failure can be one of the great teachers in life if we treat those failures as God's way of waking us up to our fullest potential. Be prepared to identify team failures and to nurture members in appropriate ways through those defeats.

WHEN IS THE CHANGE COMPLETE?

Be prepared for the transition to take a substantial amount of time—perhaps as long as two or three years. If this seems excessive, consider all that goes into the transition: redefining the role of the pastor (and staff), altering the culture of the ministry, motivating the congregation to change its roles and expectations, transitioning existing power and authority relationships, revising the lines of communication, elevating the importance of spiritual gifts and the ministry vision, and developing and implementing an entirely divergent evaluation procedure. In essence, you are reinventing your ministry. That's not going to happen overnight.

You might find that the healthier your church is, the more resistance you get from people who cling to the "If it ain't broke, don't fix it" philosophy. If your church is more than fifty years old, you are likely to meet resistance based upon the history of the church—the infamous "We've never done it that way before" mentality. If you have a relatively small contingent of powerbrokers in the body—the founding families, the major donors, the political sharks—then you may experience political maneuvering that would do the Democratic and Republican Parties proud.

If you are a leader in your church and you see the incredible potential of using a team-based approach to carrying out the vision, do not be dejected by the reluctance or outright opposition of congregants who are otherwise sane, intelligent, and savvy. Change is always painful for some, and it always comes with a price tag. Pray hard about the feasibility of converting to lay-leadership teams. When you are persuaded that the Lord will be honored by the change, prepare for the conflict that the shift will unleash and strategically present the possibilities to those who can facilitate a smooth transition. Perhaps, as several churches did, you will want to demonstrate the power of teams by appointing a team to facilitate the transition itself!

The transition will be completed when more than two-thirds of your active congregants expect all leadership provided within the church to be accomplished by teams rather than solo practitioners and when more than 80 percent of the leadership provided is actually delivered by teams rather than individuals. At that stage, realize that the momentum has swung in favor of teams, and the future of leadership in your church is not likely to revert to solo leadership without a concerted and overt effort to go backward in time. When you have reached the point of team dominance, mark it with a celebration—not because you succeeded in establishing a major transition, but because the existence of team-based leadership and a congregation that esteems teams reflects another plateau of health achieved by your church.

CHAPTER TEN

LAND MINES
IN TEAM TERRITORY

---◆◆◆---

*Be forewarned and prepare
an intelligent response
to these possible dangers.*

---◆◆◆---

No matter how carefully you plan your transition to a team-based leadership approach, you will undoubtedly experience significant challenges along the way. Based on our exploration of the process that many team-based churches have undertaken, allow me to identify some of those land mines that await your arrival. The types of challenges might be categorized as those related to:

- providing consistency in leadership

- the appropriate allocation of leadership and ministry resources

- introducing and maintaining appropriate processes for team leadership

- handling people's unrealistic or harmful expectations

Be forewarned and prepare an intelligent response to these possible dangers.

CHALLENGES RELATED TO CONSISTENCY IN LEADERSHIP

Leaders are people who take risks, but the nature of the leadership they provide must have a high degree of predictability and consistency if followers are to remain confident in and devoted to their leaders. Consider some of the difficulties leaders will face regarding the ability to provide consistent leadership.

Lacking the Motivation

When you were young, you probably believed that your parents never got tired of being parents and that they needed no encouragement to continue in that role. It may have seemed as if their only purpose on earth was to be your mother and father and that no amount of positive reinforcement would alter their commitment to or fulfillment derived from that task.

Christians tend to treat church leaders the same way as kids treat their parents: We assume that church leaders get such immeasurable pleasure and satisfaction from the practice of leading that they need no applause or commendations. How wrong that sentiment is! Even though leading is sometimes an enjoyable function for those who are called to it, it can also be taxing and thankless. Leaders are human too and need to receive occasional indications that their efforts are significant and producing worthwhile results. Because a church's lay leaders do not receive any financial remuneration for their efforts, the compensation they derive is psychological and emotional. How can you facilitate such support for their efforts?

First, help them remain focused on the vision of their team. The vision was the outcome that initially sparked their passion and motivated them to dive into the fray. If leaders truly grasp God's vision for their lives and ministry and understand how it connects with the vision of the team and how the pursuit of that vision will bolster the impact and wholeness of the church, the chances of their becoming blasé about God's vision are minimal. Leaders are vision-driven people. Keeping them focused on the incredible influence of God's vision stokes a true leader's passion to deliver whatever it takes to bring that potential to reality.

> *What can be done to build a churchwide culture that esteems and affirms its leaders on a regular basis?*

Second, a few words and gestures of sincere appreciation and encouragement go a long way toward restoring the energy and commitment of leaders. While a great leader does not live for personal compliments and external rewards, all human beings are moved by kind words and tangible expressions of gratitude. What can you do to stimulate your congregation to develop the habit of passing on heartfelt expressions of thanks for the life-changing labor of the church's leaders? Rather than taking leaders for granted, what can be done to build a churchwide culture that esteems and affirms its leaders on a regular basis?

Third, have you created mechanisms that allow leaders to come in contact with individuals whose lives have been changed by the work of the leader's team? Personal testimonies of impact lift the spirits of leaders faster than anything else I've seen. A collection of testimonies may not represent a valid assessment of the impact and quality of a team's ministry, but stories of how lives have changed often make leaders feel that the time and effort they have sacrificed on behalf of the ministry—time spent away from family, time drawn from leisure, time devoted to ministry after long, hard days at their jobs—is paying off in eternal dividends.

Finally, there is value to pointing leaders back toward the initial reason for their involvement on the team: the sense that God called them to lead and that their leadership is a central facet of their personal service to Jesus Christ. What other endeavor could possibly bring resonant, lasting fulfillment to a leader than to fulfill that calling? Discouragement and fatigue are enemies of every leader, and during such times a leader may wistfully dream about other ministry opportunities. Sometimes it is helpful to play out a scenario of the "greener pasture" to underscore how unfulfilling such a transition would be. We draw our greatest satisfaction from those things to which God has called us; sometimes we need to be reminded of that principle.

Burning Out Your People

What happens in your ministry when you find a good leader? In many churches, that individual is used as often and as broadly as possible. "Good leaders are hard to find. When I find one, I use him wherever he can be useful," admitted one pastor we interviewed. Doesn't that create problems such as burnout, being spread too thin, lacking deep passion for the ministries in which he gets involved? "Yeah, I suppose so, but we need help. I can't worry about his being burned out tomorrow when I've got fires to put out today. If I have a leader, what choice do I have but to use him where he's needed, when he's needed?"

There is the danger that the same philosophy—essentially using the leader as a jack-of-all-trades troubleshooter—will be adopted in a team-leadership environment. In practical terms, you might be tempted to allow or even encourage your best leaders to serve on two or three teams simultaneously or to move them from place to place to patch holes or shake up dormant teams.

Take a tip from the churches that have perfected the art of lay-leadership teams: Limit your leaders to one team at a time, and let them focus on the team whose vision released their passion. Such a limitation may produce temporary hardships while you search for additional leaders to join nascent or rebuilt teams, but the long-term benefits will justify the short-term pain. Your leaders will last longer, thus enhancing the value of the team on which they serve, and increasing the benefit to the church. Leaders will be more effective and add greater value to the ministry by being able to focus all of their energy and abilities on the challenges facing one team, rather than suffering from distraction and divided loyalties by serving on multiple teams simultaneously. They are also likely to appreciate the opportunity to invest fully in the vision that stokes their passion, rather than simply serving on multiple teams where natural skills and past experiences make them solid if uninspired contributors.

Don't be surprised if you encounter a few leaders who ask to serve on two or more teams at the same time. Many capable leaders are energetic, impatient, and self-confident. More than a few also savor the prospect of being able to "save" failing ministries. Be sure that someone in the ministry has a clear understanding of the importance of saying no to requests to serve in multiple capacities at once and has the authority to enforce that policy. No matter how silly such a rule may seem at the outset, years of experience in team-led churches across the nation have verified the value of helping the most aggressive lay leaders narrow their sights and channel their capacity to the productivity of one team.

Replacing Lost Leaders

One of the disappointing experiences of lay-team leadership is watching a great team lose a key member. The reasons for such losses run the gamut from the unpredictable (death, illness, job relocation) to the disheartening (moral failure, divorce) to the foolish (burnout). Some turnover is unavoidable. How your church handles these situations will determine the ultimate viability of the team.

Regardless of the reason for the departure of a valued member, the team must be allowed to grieve the loss. That process requires time, some internal "space," and emotional sensitivity. The more closely knit the team becomes, the more like a family it behaves. Just as a family would have to work through the impact of losing one of its members, so must a healthy team invest significant time and energy in addressing the emotional, spiritual, intellectual, and productivity implications of the loss.

Most teams will choose to continue despite the transition—and rightly so. Because good teams do not hinge on the presence or absence of a single individual, it is more plausible to replace a team member who is removed from the leadership mix than to replace a high-profile solo leader who leaves the scene. There will be a time of adjustment necessary as the team integrates a new leader to replace the departed colleague. Although the team will rely upon the relationships and other internal strengths that have been built up over time, it will take time and intentional effort to redefine the team's nature and relationships with the new, incoming partner.

To help prepare for the turnover contingency, many successful team-led churches have initiated "apprenticeship" programs in which an apprentice is available to assist the affected team. While that person is not likely to be a carbon copy of the lost member, moving the departed leader's apprentice into the team's open slot will smooth the transition. The team may handle the presence of the apprentice in various ways, such as treating his or her assistance as a temporary fix until a more permanent replacement can be identified and invited or "trying out" the apprentice as a potential permanent replacement. Either way, the apprentice helps the team continue to provide effective leadership until the long-term direction of the team is determined.

Disbanding the Successful Team

Sometimes the best advice is counterintuitive. An example of such counsel is to disband a team that has successfully fulfilled its vision.

Why would a church voluntarily break up a unit that has proven its capacity to serve effectively? The heart of the issue relates to the purpose for the team's existence—namely, to fulfill the vision. The vision is what attracted these individuals to that particular team. The vision is what ignited their passion. So once the vision has been brought to reality, the team may no longer have a reason to exist.

It is sometimes difficult for organizations to accept the idea that every relationship has a definable life cycle. A team created for the purpose of accomplishing a specified outcome loses its reason for being once that outcome has come to fruition. Disbanding that team is not an admission of failure but a sign of the ministry's maturity.

Would assigning the team to a new vision or allowing it to create a new role for itself better serve the ministry? The answer is usually no. Insisting that the team hang on beyond its time can undermine the vitality and impact of the group. The best strategy is to celebrate the success of the team, officially dissolve the collective, and encourage leaders to discern where God wants them to serve next. Acknowledging the value that the team has provided, while helping each individual to get a fresh start on a new team, will keep each leader invigorated and productive.

Realistically, God's vision for a church or a team is not something that is accomplished quickly. The vision usually takes years of concentrated, faithful effort before it becomes reality. In many cases a team will be together for a decade or more. Sometimes the vision outlives the team. When the team, however, has reached the top of its mountain, it may choose to search the landscape for new challenges to pursue, or it may sense a need to stay together to build on the vision that it has helped bring to reality.

When the Transitioning Pastor Transitions Out

Leading a church from solo leadership to team leadership takes time, a comprehensive process, congregational trust in its leaders, a commitment to making teams successful, and a transitional leader. The transitional leader is sometimes a gifted layperson, pastoral associate, or staff person, but usually it is the senior pastor. Facilitating the shift to team leadership may well be the crowning organizational achievement of the pastor's ministry career.

For that transition to be successful, however, the pastor must be at the church long enough to complete the transition and to nurture it through the first year or two after the change has been implemented. Some denominations regularly move pastors from one church to another, and moving a pastor who is in the midst of a transition process can cripple the church for many years to come by removing the process champion in midstream. In other cases (although this has been rare) the senior pastor decides to retire or change pastorates in the midst of the transition. In still other instances, the church gets immersed in the transition and then changes its mind—effectively closing down the process by firing its pastor. Any of these situations will severely harm the church.

If you serve a denomination that reassigns pastors, covenant with the denomination to allow you to remain with your church until the transition is completed. If the denomination is not willing to make such an agreement, you have two alternatives: Mentor a layperson to spearhead the shift or postpone the transition until there is sufficient leadership stability to complete the transaction.

If you are a pastor who would be the primary leader of a move to teams, but you are not totally committed to being at your church for the next four or five years, you can still lay the foundation for your successor to make the shift. One of your greatest parting gifts to the congregation would be to prepare them for the transition without initiating it prematurely.

If you are the pastor who will spearhead the shift to teams, be sure to acquire the support of key influencers within the congregation prior to instigating the change. Undoubtedly there will be a few laypersons whose sense of power, authority, and prominence will be undermined by the shift. Work with your base of supporters to ensure that threatened or potentially disgruntled individuals do not hinder what is best for the church.

ALLOCATION OF RESOURCES

The allocation of resources is another potential minefield in the transition to lay-team leadership. There is a natural tendency for people—especially leaders—to desire more authority, more power, more budget, more people, more responsibility, more of just about everything. How ministry resources are allocated can produce astounding breakthroughs—or shatter the strength and focus of teams, bringing the ministry down with them. Be alert to the following potential problem areas.

Driving the Communications Process

Some churches expect their lay leaders to drive the communications process that exists between the pastor/staff and leadership team. "We're full-time ministry professionals," explained one pastor at a church that was struggling with its team process. "If the team wants information or other resources, they know where to find us. We are very comfortable waiting for them to initiate contact."

> *When push comes to shove, the clergy are on the payroll to enable the efforts of the congregation.*

A more sensible and fruitful strategy is to expect the full-time ministry professionals to direct the communications flow with each of the church's leadership teams. Although some people might see things differently, the most reasonable perspective is to acknowledge that the pastor and staff exist to serve the ministry efforts of the laity. Thousands of churches are suffering today because they have that relationship backward, expecting the laity to do whatever they can to facilitate the ministry of the paid professionals. The ideal situation is a positive, intimate, symbiotic relationship between the clergy and laity, but when push comes to shove, the clergy are on the payroll to enable the efforts of the congregation.

As employees of the ministry, the pastor and staff likely have better access to information and resources that will help each leadership team do its job most effectively. Consequently, it makes sense for the pastor and staff to take the initiative to stay in touch with the team, to divulge information that would help them, to facilitate the provision of existing resources for their work, and to regularly debrief the team to determine how the church might best support their future efforts. Expecting the team to perform this function invites misunderstanding and disaster.

Stockpiling Talent

Leaders attract leaders, and winners attract everybody. Undoubtedly, at some point you will face a situation in which one particular team begins to hoard leaders. This is the church equivalent of a championship sports team stockpiling talented players who will forfeit their ability to make gobs of money on lesser teams for the chance to play with a winner. One of your lay teams will likely emerge as a superior blend of talents, no matter how low-key, humble, or servant-oriented they may be. Other leaders may strive to get attached to that team, even as apprentices or "second string" leaders, simply for the joy of being where the action is and experiencing success after success.

This spectacle has the potential to destroy all of your teams. First, when leaders run to a team because of its success, they lose sight of the most important motivation for joining one: the team's vision. Second, when one or a handful of teams is allowed to bank talent for future use, the church will suffer in the immediate term by not having access to the leaders God has provided for the present day. Third, stockpiled leaders will lose the opportunity to experience the joy of serving and growing at an optimal pace. Instead, they will watch others serve while they simmer in the minor leagues. Fourth, envy of certain teams will breed jealousy, infighting, and other unhealthy attitudes and behaviors.

One of the most intriguing qualities of the successful team-led ministries we observed is that they disallow stockpiling—even when they are blessed with an abundance of leaders. Instead, these churches engage in rampant innovation, moving unassigned leaders onto new teams. You can never have enough leaders, and you will never have too many leaders, if you orchestrate their interaction to permit creative partnerships and entrepreneurial activity. You might consider prohibiting putting leadership talent "on ice" as a breach of church values. Allow each team to gather the human resources it needs, then direct additional talented individuals to other opportunities within the ministry.

THE TEAM LEADERSHIP DEVELOPMENT PROCESS

No matter how great an idea team leadership may be, you can count on the transition from solo leadership to team-based leadership to stir significant dissension and controversy. From those who figure to lose some degree of autonomy and power to those who resist dismantling the way things have always been or who simply hate change, prepare yourself for some lively discussions and savvy politicking. Good things never come easily; a shift from solo-based leadership to team-based leadership will prove the point. You may wish to prepare for some of the following barriers to a smooth transition.

> *The groups most commonly requesting such untouchable status are the elders and the deacons.*

Untouchable Teams

During the transition from solo-based leadership to team-based leadership you will undoubtedly encounter a few people who suggest that the team process be adopted but the existing "teams" be "grandfathered" into the new system. In other words, existing groups of individuals who fill a leadership capacity in the church may want to be exempted from the fresh approach by virtue of their existence prior to the new systems. We found that the groups most commonly requesting such untouchable status are the elders and the deacons.

If you cave in to such demands, you are asking for severe headaches in the near future. As you seek to develop a church culture that proclaims team leadership to be the only acceptable approach to leading the church, permitting preexisting exceptions will undermine this new culture and the potential for your teams. Many pastors have argued that their elders and deacons are already serving as a leadership team. In my experience, however, most elders and deacons are not leaders; those groups are too large to operate as effective teams. They are not wed to a common vision that brought them together in the first place, and they do not have complementary leadership aptitudes that facilitate ministry efficacy. I am not arguing for the elimination of elders and deacons. Rather, I am arguing for philosophical and practical consistency in how your church is led. Maintain a board of elders or deacons, but reduce its size to make it a manageable group of true leaders who reflect the demeanor of leadership teams.

At some point in your transition from solo leadership to team leadership you will encounter the conflict with traditions. This may well be the place to address the role of traditional behavior and thinking: How should the eldership of the church be handled? Typically, you will fight battles concerning a reduction in the number of elders, the revisions in the core criteria for selecting elders, and the very purpose of elders within the church. Rather than a group of individuals who merely have a significant history at the church and a true affection for it, the elders should be the chief leadership council of the church—a small group of leaders who focus on the aggregate ministry and spiritual health of the congregation.

For some churches, this reflects no change at all, but for most congregations, this approach represents a radical and wrenching shift in direction, policy, practice, and perspective. If you choose to use teams, be prepared for this battle.

Infiltration by the Professionals

In many churches the rule is that every team must include at least one pastor or staff person. In some cases I have seen churches require that a pastor or staffer be the team captain. It usually doesn't take too much digging to discover that this is a reflection of the church professionals' desire to maintain control of the ministry and to retain a significant influence over all decisions.

Again, we need to distinguish between macro-level and micro-level teams. At the macro-level (teams that provide comprehensive leadership to the totality of the church) it may be deemed entirely appropriate to invite a pastor onto that team. At the micro-level (teams that lead specific dimensions of the aggregate ministry, such as the worship ministry, the outreach ministry, the Christian education ministry), however, it is less advisable to incorporate clergy and church professionals onto the teams unless absolutely necessary.

There are times—particularly in situations of crisis, a small church just beginning a team process, or where the pastor or staff person has extraordinary expertise—that assigning a pastor or staff person to a team makes perfect sense. Generally speaking, though, populating each ministry team with qualified, passionate laypeople is preferable to mixing staff and laity. Pastors and staff may most profitably serve as advisors to one or more teams, and there may be times when the experience and knowledge of those individuals encourages a team to annex that person for a period of time in what amounts to a consulting capacity.

Avoiding the Apprenticeship

Churches with successful teams incorporate an apprenticeship process. But many potential apprentices may balk at the thought of playing second fiddle to any other person in the church—especially if the would-be apprentice has an impressive leadership résumé. The value of the apprenticeship is manifold: It gives the newcomer a sense of the operating culture of the ministry, introduces him or her to the leadership style and quirks of the church, and provides an opportunity to become more comfortable with the divisions of responsibility.

One of the most beneficial by-products of the apprenticeship, though, is the demonstration of humility and servanthood signaled by one's willingness to work through the established process, regardless of personal experience or capacity. In one of the churches we studied, a fifty-four-year-old senior vice president of a Fortune 500 company joined the church and, after a period of time, was invited to participate as a leader. His first opportunity was to serve as an apprentice to a thirty-one-year-old auto mechanic who had served as a leader at the church for five years. When the accomplished businessman refused to do so, explaining that he had more experience and leadership wisdom than the younger, less educated man who would be his mentor, the church withdrew its offer.

> *One of the most beneficial by-products of the apprenticeship is the demonstration of humility and servanthood.*

"It was quite tense," recalled the senior leader of the team to which the executive had been invited. "There is no doubt that John [the ex-ecutive] had incredible experience and abilities. He had proven his skill level in the business world. In fact, his record of accomplishments was one of the things that caused us to want him to help us lead the church forward. He obviously had a lot of training and abilities that could help us.

"But our thought was that if John couldn't humble himself long enough to become a servant of someone who loves Christ and has a track record of good leadership in our church, then he wasn't spiritually mature enough to be a leader. We think of leadership as serving people, not ordering them around and producing results at any cost. Our culture here is different than at [the executive's company], and I don't think John was ready to make that transition."

> *When expectations are out of line with reality, the change is doomed from the start.*

Inflexibility of Team Activity

Great teams must remain internally flexible. For instance, sometimes a *strategic leader* may have to temporarily provide operational leadership for the team while the *operational leader* is focused on an all-consuming effort that precludes personal involvement in other aspects of the team's work at that time. Or the *team-building leader* may have to serve as the *directing leader* while the latter is unavailable due to other commitments to the team. This is why it is so important for all of the team's members to learn from one another and to be constantly growing in their personal leadership capacity. While team theory permits us to cleanly differentiate and separate the responsibilities and activities of each team member, team reality shows no respect for those divisions of labor. The more comfortable each team member becomes covering for a teammate, without trying to take over his or her area of emphasis, the more effective the team will be in its mission.

UNREALISTIC OR HARMFUL EXPECTATIONS

Any time a major change is made within a ministry, people expect certain results. Sometimes those expectations are reasonable, but sometimes they are not. When expectations are out of line with reality, the change is doomed from the start. Yet you do not want people's expectations to be so low that they lack excitement or enthusiasm related to the alteration being implemented. What are people's expectations of your solo leaders? How would those expectations change if you shift to lay teams to provide direction for the ministry? How appropriate are those expectations?

Demanding Too Much Too Soon

Switching from solo leadership to team-based leadership represents a huge transformation in church culture, ministry process, authority allocation, and people's thinking. A great transition process will get the congregation excited about the possibilities and have them anxiously anticipating the shift to a more effective, efficient, and productive leadership paradigm. Because people are uncomfortable with change and are increasingly skeptical of the claims of superiority regarding new products, services, or procedures, one of the pressures the transition team will face is that of producing results—quickly, broadly, perfectly, and undeniably.

You may discover that the deeper the opposition to team-based leadership, the higher the initial expectations your opponents will set for the new approach. Instead of acknowledging and applauding improvements in practice and results, opponents will complain that the new approach has failed to produce perfection. Instead of appreciating the fact that more people are using their gifts and producing great ministry outcomes, detractors will focus on the fact that most people are not serving as leaders in the expanded leadership approach. Rather than celebrate greater efficiencies realized through leadership teams, resistance will be waged on the basis of the amount of time and energy that was devoted to the transition itself.

As you might imagine, conceding to the pressure to produce big results too quickly can completely destroy well-developed plans, growing momentum, and small victories that eventually lead to significant gains. What can you do to protect the transition process from demands that you produce big results quickly? Consider six recommendations:

1. *Before you initiate the process of change, gather your facts regarding the compelling reasons for the transition—* including the harsh realities concerning the inefficiency and ineffectiveness of solo leadership at your church. Hopefully, these statistics, anecdotes, and behavioral patterns will not have to be used in a confrontation regarding the need for the transition—but it will be helpful to have those facts readily available should they be needed.

2. *From the start, monitor and modify people's expectations of what the transition will produce* so that people's assumptions and hopes are reasonable. Examine how quickly they expect results, how much upheaval they anticipate as the church moves to a team-based culture, and what they believe each leader or team will produce. When their expectations are out of sync with reality, confront them and provide a more reasonable concept of likely results.

3. *Do not launch into the process until you have consensus among all of the church's key leaders* that team-based leadership is best for the church—and that the inevitable challenges and discomfort brought on by the transition will be compensated for by the enhanced ministry outcomes that result.

4. *Begin the process with a pilot team* whose experience will quietly and unobtrusively test the waters and help identify unexpected or unaddressed challenges regarding the process, the people, or the productivity of the team approach within your church. By starting out small and outside of the scrutiny of the congregation, you will increase the chances of success when the process is expanded.

5. Once you have initiated the team process, do not hesitate to *encourage congregants by pointing out the small,*

day-to-day victories achieved by your teams. People do not usually argue with successful outcomes. The more they sense that the team strategy is producing as desired and that there is momentum building behind the team approach, the less likely they will be to mount an offensive against the new way of doing things.

6. *Get everyone involved in the process.* People feel a deeper sense of ownership when they are significantly involved in facilitating a meaningful ministry change. Those who own the process will be less prone to bad-mouthing it or refusing to acknowledge its value to the church. There are many possible avenues for assistance with the team transition, but one of the most powerful and useful is for nonleader congregants to pray for both the process and for the individuals involved in the process. Only a spiritually dysfunctional individual would pray for a specific group and outcome, and then work to undermine the prayed-for outcomes through gossip, complaining, or political maneuvering.

Naturally, even when the transition produces results, there will be bumps and bruises along the way. Be ready to address the concerns of individuals whose support for teams is tenuous. They are not bad people but simply scared and lack a full understanding of the vision and value of teams. Help them stay focused, trusting, and supportive.

A Dearth of Teams

In some small churches, pastors worry that they do not have enough leaders to develop a wide range of teams. Sometimes the problem is not knowing what types of people to look for as leaders, which may lead to vain searches for superheroes. In other situations the problem is not the lack of leaders but that the church is trying to do too much. Once the church develops a reasonable plan for growing its ministry capacity, then it can unleash teams on an as-needed or as-available basis.

Resist the temptation to assign any given team to double duty in which it takes on two or more dimensions of the ministry. As noted earlier, when individual leaders serve on two or more teams, the energy, passion, vision, and resources of the team become compromised, resulting in unsatisfying results.

OTHER LAND MINES ALONG THE WAY

Our research identified many other land mines that await churches moving into a team process. Hopefully, your understanding of the philosophy behind the choices described above, as well as the concept of team-based lay leadership outlined in previous chapters, will prepare you to intelligently and strategically respond to other challenges that may emerge as you pursue team leadership. Be assured: If you stay the course and address problems promptly and resolutely, the ministry results in your church will be well worth the effort.

CHAPTER ELEVEN

A SELF-EXAMINATION

—————◆◆◆—————

*Solo leadership
or team leadership:
Which option is best for you?*

—————◆◆◆—————

Occasionally life's choices are either-or propositions: Either you choose one option, or you are left with the other. Americans dislike having such limited choices. We prefer the sense of control and power, as well as the pleasure, of having truly disparate alternatives from a broad range of possibilities.

In choosing your leadership approach—solo leadership or team leadership—it appears that you have an either-or challenge. Which option is best for you? As you consider your answer, keep the following observations in mind:

- Churches can grow only as much as their leaders will facilitate. The degree of growth made possible by teams of gifted
  leaders working together will generally exceed the growth
  feasible under a group of solo leaders.

- The more a church allows leaders to use their gifts and skills for ministry, the more leaders the church will attract and retain. The more leaders the church attracts and retains, the more likely the church is to develop a full-orbed, healthy ministry.

Churches can grow only as much
as their leaders will facilitate.

- It seems most likely that God's design for leadership is for individuals to work together in teams—and thus minimize personal glory—than for a single, solo leader to strive to make everything happen and receive the brunt of the church's attention. Team leadership helps keep the focus on God, while solo leadership may deflect the spotlight from Him.

- When personnel changes happen, a church is less likely to be crippled by the departure of one team member than by the departure of the solo leader. The church will struggle in both situations, but the struggle will be less profound in the case of losing one team-based leader.

- Quality in leadership is enhanced by constant and objective performance evaluation. Solo leaders have a relatively poor track record of self-evaluation when compared to the self-assessment of leadership teams.

• In a solo-leadership model, the qualification standards may be high but the production standards are often unmet. In a team-leadership model, the qualification standards are not as lofty but the productivity level is typically met or exceeded. The question for a church is whether it is more interested in impressing people with the quality of a single or small number of leaders or in the quality and ministry impact of what a larger number of team-based leaders produces.

Team-based leadership—utilizing the wealth of talents and abilities that God has invested in laypeople—is not the answer to every challenge and dilemma facing the church. The continued refusal to exploit those talents and abilities, however, leaves churches at a disadvantage. The team approach may not solve every problem, but it often increases the potential for eliminating many of the vexing issues that perplex churches large and small.

Which Way Is Right for You?

To arrive at the best choice for your church, you might take an inventory of how your leadership process and output is presently faring. I encourage you to prayerfully answer the following questions and reflect on whether team leadership or solo leadership is likely to facilitate improvements in the ministry impact of your church.

1. What is the vision for your church's ministry? How widely known and owned is that vision among your congregants?

2. What goals have you set in the past year in relation to your vision? How satisfactorily did your church meet all of those goals?

3. Is the senior pastor of your church a true leader? How well does he or she work with and develop other leaders? Would the pastor's productivity and personal well-being improve if your leadership model shifted?

4. What is your church's philosophy of leadership and leadership development? How confident are you that your philosophy is an ideal match with your congregation's needs?

5. How does your church identify potential lay leaders? How viable is that approach?

6. Once lay leaders are identified, what happens with them? What types of preparation and development do your lay leaders receive? How many of them voluntarily stay heavily involved as leaders for an extended period of service?

7. How do you ascertain the leadership aptitudes of your leaders? If you identify those distinctions, how do you apply that knowledge to the assignments given to your leaders?

8. Does your church culture foster team leadership or solo leadership? Is that intentional?

9. How many lay leaders have left your church because they felt that their gifts would never be adequately or appropriately used? How many lay leaders have left your church because they were burned out by your ministry?

10. How difficult is it to keep your lay leaders motivated to stay sharp and involved?

11. How does your church evaluate the effectiveness of its leaders? How effective is that evaluation process? How could it be improved?

12. Which approach would be of greatest benefit to your church: solo leadership or team leadership? If your church were to transition from one to the other, what price would be paid for that change? In what ways would the results be worth the price?

Whether you determine that lay-leadership teams or solo-based leadership is the best path for your church to pursue, my prayer is that you will empower every leader God has brought to your church to live up to his or her ministry and leadership potential. And all things being equal, I pray that your church will strongly consider the merits and benefits of employing lay-leadership teams as your strategy for unleashing God's greatest blessings upon your ministry and those whom it will influence.

NOTES

Chapter One: Are We Setting Up Pastors—
and Churches—for Failure?

1. This survey was a nationwide, random sample survey of 1,005 adults conducted in July 1996 by the Barna Research Group, Ltd.

2. This book discusses the social and spiritual trends and responses that characterize America, including our predictions of what the country will be like at the end of this decade. We have endeavored to describe the implications of these changes and how Christians might reasonably respond to these challenges. See George Barna and Mark Hatch, *Boiling Point* (Ventura, Calif.: Regal, 2001).

Chapter Two: Why Team Leadership?

1. Vision is a clear and compelling mental portrait of a preferable future that God communicates to His chosen people. Vision is about change, purpose, focus, and obedience to God. Without vision, there is no leadership. For Christians, one of the challenges is to pursue God's vision, not a person's own vision for the future. A leader is

successful when he or she is effectively enabling people to pursue (and ultimately fulfill) the vision entrusted to the people by God.

Chapter Three: Without Vision, There Is No Leadership

1. A national survey we conducted among a random sample of 602 senior pastors of Protestant churches revealed that less than one out of every twenty pastors was able to identify God's vision for his or her church's ministry. A concurrent survey conducted among a national sample of more than 400 born-again Christians showed that an even smaller proportion of believers was able to articulate God's vision for their life and ministry.

2. I have written much more extensively on mission, vision, and values in previous books. For greater detail on vision in ministry, consult *Turning Vision into Action* (Ventura, Calif.: Regal, 1996); *The Power of Vision* (Ventura, Calif.: Regal, 1992); and chapter 3 of *Leaders on Leadership* (Ventura, Calif.: Regal, 1997).

3. Additional discussion of the relationship of these elements to one another and to ministry is provided in my previous book, *Church Marketing: Breaking Ground for the Harvest* (Ventura, Calif.: Regal, 1992).

4. The names have been changed to protect the church's privacy.

Chapter Four: Why Teams Are Scarce (and Why They Shouldn't Be)

1. Peter Drucker, *Managing the Non-Profit Organization* (New York: HarperCollins, 1990), 122-5.

2. Peter writes of the priesthood of believers in 1 Peter 2:5-6,9. John addresses this in Revelation 1:5-6; 5:9-10; and 20:6.

Chapter Six: The Four Leadership Aptitudes

1. Perhaps you are wondering how to easily determine a person's leadership aptitude without having to rely upon trial and error. In 2001, upon the completion of the beta testing phase, Barna Research will be releasing the Ministry Leader Profile, a self-administered diagnostic tool that will help individuals to evaluate their leadership potential. The tool will explore a person's calling, character, competencies, and leadership aptitude. For information about the availability of this resource, check http://www.barna.org, the Barna Research Group Web site.

Chapter Seven: "Best Practices" of Successful Team Leadership

1. There are two ways in which satellite-based training is available these days. One option is to experience the singular, topical events broadcast by ministries such as Willow Creek Community Church, Saddleback Community Church, and Injoy. An alternative that delivers valuable continuity and breadth is provided by organizations like the Church Communications Network, which offers a series of monthly or bimonthly broadcasts on topics of interest to church leaders as well as special pay-per-view types of training events. More information on CCN's programming can be obtained from their Web site (http://www.ccnonline.net) or by calling 1-800-321-6781.

Chapter Nine: Transitioning to a Team-Led Ministry

1. You may notice that what I have suggested is lay-leadership teams focused around the six pillars of the church as described in Acts as well as in my previous book, *The Habits of Highly Effective Churches*. To facilitate effective leadership teams, build them around the basic foundations of your church's ministry however you choose to organize it. Each "department" or "division" of the ministry should interact with its own focused team. For more insight into the notion of organizing around the six pillars, see *The Habits of Highly Effective Churches* (Ventura, Calif.: Regal, 2000).

BIBLIOGRAPHY

Anderson, Leith. *Leadership That Works*. Minneapolis: Bethany, 1999.

Barna, George. *Church Marketing: Breaking Ground for the Harvest*. Ventura, Calif.: Regal, 1992.

———. *Effective Lay Leadership Teams*. Ventura, Calif.: Issachar Resources, 2000.

———. *The Habits of Highly Effective Churches*. Ventura, Calif.: Regal, 2000.

———. *The Power of Vision*. Ventura, Calif.: Regal, 1992.

———. *The Second Coming of the Church*. Nashville: Word, 1998.

———. *Turning Vision into Action*. Ventura, Calif.: Regal, 1996.

———, ed. *Leaders on Leadership*. Ventura, Calif.: Regal, 1997.

Cladis, George. *Leading the Team-Based Church*. San Francisco: Jossey-Bass, 1999.

Cordeiro, Wayne. *Doing Church As a Team.* Honolulu: New Hope Resources, 1998.

Gangel, Kenneth. *Team Leadership in Christian Ministry.* Chicago: Moody, 1997.

Heenan, David, and Warren Bennis. *Co-Leaders.* New York: Wiley, 1999.

Katzenbach, Jon, ed. *The Work of Teams.* Boston: Harvard Business School Publishing, 1998.

————, and Douglas Smith. *The Wisdom of Teams.* New York: Harper Business, 1993.

Thrall, Bill, Bruce McNicol, and Ken McElrath. *The Ascent of a Leader.* San Francisco: Jossey-Bass, 1999.

Wilkes, C. Gene. *Jesus on Leadership.* Wheaton, Ill.: Tyndale, 1998.

ACKNOWLEDGMENTS

———— ⬥ ————

Most of the books I have written have been a joy to produce, with ideas flooding my mind and words exploding onto the page, the result making sense even in the earliest drafts. This book has been the exception to that history. In spite of my passion to see godly leadership within the church and my zealous belief in the notion of team leadership, my writing schedule and frustrations put several people through unfortunate torture. I'd like to ask their forgiveness, thank them for their patience, and applaud their perseverance.

The person who suffered the most has been my wife. Nancy held on as best she could, trying to carve out more and more time for me to sequester myself in hotel rooms and other available places, playing both mother and father to the girls during my labored writing days. This was especially difficult while we were traveling during our seminar tour, as I struggled to capture the proper focus and energy to write between travel days and speaking engagements. She is an incredible woman and a tremendous helper. My gratitude is also extended to my daughters, Samantha and Corban, who came in a close second in the abandonment contest. My buddies again forfeited Daddy several days too many and, at times, when it was just plain unfair to do so. They rebounded with characteristic sympathy and enthusiasm. Thank you, girls, for loving me, praying for me and for this book every night, and for believing that we will schedule my time better in the future. You deserve nothing less.

I put my team at Barna Research through some tough times as a result of this book, too. Rachel Ables good-naturedly endured my missed deadlines, cheerfully juggled her other duties without complaint, and masterfully produced the first edition of this book. David Kinnaman expertly ran the company during my absence. Meg Wells, Pam Jacob, Carmen Moore, Jill Kinnaman, Irene Robles, Celeste Rivera, Julie Carobini, and Kim Wilson all flexed without grumbling and kept the ministry moving forward without missing a beat. I have been blessed with a great team of leaders and ministers whose efforts continue to bless me and thousands around the world.

As always, it has been a privilege to serve God and His people through the writing of another book. The hardships I bore in the process are not worthy of being mentioned in the same breath as those that Jesus suffered because of my sins. My prayer is that He will use this offering as a vehicle to assist other servants in the ministry. To Him alone belongs the glory.

ABOUT GEORGE BARNA

George Barna is the president of The Barna Research Group, Ltd., a marketing research firm located in Ventura, California. The company specializes in conducting primary research for Christian ministries and nonprofit organizations. Since its inception in 1984, Barna Research has served several hundred parachurch ministries and numerous churches in addition to various nonprofit and for-profit organizations.

Barna is a prolific author. His most recent works include *The Power of Team Leadership, Growing True Disciples, Boiling Point,* and *The Habits of Highly Effective Churches.* Past works include bestsellers such as *The Frog in the Kettle, The Second Coming of the Church, User Friendly Churches, Marketing the Church,* and *The Power of Vision.* Several of his books have received national awards. He has also written for numerous periodicals and has published more than two-dozen syndicated reports on a variety of topics related to ministry. His work is frequently cited as an authoritative source by the media.

Barna is also widely known for his intensive, research-based seminars for church leaders. He is a popular speaker at ministry conferences around the world and has taught at several universities and seminaries. He has served as a pastor of a large, multi-ethnic church and has served on several boards of directors. He is the founding director of The Barna Institute, a nonprofit organization dedicated to providing strategic information to ministries.

After graduating summa cum laude with a degree in sociology from Boston College, Barna earned two master's degrees from Rutgers University. He also received a doctorate from Dallas Baptist University.

He lives with his wife, Nancy, and their two daughters, Samantha and Corban, in Southern California. He enjoys spending time with his family, writing, reading, playing basketball and guitar, relaxing on the beach, and visiting bookstores.

About The Barna
Research Group, Ltd.

———— ◆◆◆ ————

The Barna Research Group, Ltd. (BRG) is a full-service marketing research company in Ventura, California. BRG has been providing information and analysis regarding cultural trends, ministry practices, marketing and business strategy, fund-raising, worldviews, and leadership since 1984. The vision of the company is to provide Christian ministries with current, accurate, and reliable information in bite-sized pieces and at affordable prices to facilitate effective and strategic decision making.

BRG conducts both quantitative and qualitative research using a variety of data collection methods, with particular emphasis on the application of the results. The company conducts more research within the Christian community than any other organization in the United States and regularly releases reports describing its findings regarding the values, attitudes, lifestyles, religious beliefs and religious practices of adults and teenagers, and the current state of churches. That information is also accessible through the seminars, books, tapes, and a Web site produced by BRG.

To access many of the findings of BRG, visit the company's Web site at http://www.barna.org. You will have access to the free bimonthly reports (*The Barna Update*) published on the site, a data archive that provides current statistics in relation to forty aspects of ministry and lifestyle, the various resources produced by George Barna and The Barna Research Group, and information about upcoming seminars as well as the firm's research activities. If you wish to receive *The Barna Update* by e-mail every two weeks, you may sign up for that free service on the home page of the site.

To contact The Barna Research Group, call 805-658-8885 or write to 5528 Everglades Street, Ventura, CA 93003.

Don't miss George Barna's
special report for Christian leaders:

Growing True Disciples
New Strategies for Producing Genuine Followers of Christ

Available at bookstores everywhere.

Printed in the United States
by Baker & Taylor Publisher Services